Conte[...]

...NSORSHIP
VOLUME 43 NUMBER 01

Culture

ARTS COUNCIL ENGLAND
Supported using public funding by
ARTS COUNCIL
ENGLAND

Line out

by **Rachael Jolley**

EDITORIAL

43(1): 3/5 | DOI: 10.1177/0306422014525895

THE YIN AND yang of communication in wartime; censorship and propaganda are the positive and negative of the same idea; telling official stories and drawing out unofficial ones.

As we approach the centenary of the beginning of World War I, the time to examine the role of propaganda, communication and censorship during conflicts could not be more appropriate. The word propaganda in the sense we use it today first came into use during the WWI period. Before then, the word was mainly used in a religious, particularly Catholic context, and not necessarily with the negative overtones we associate with its modern definition; previously its context was about increasing knowledge.

That's not to say propaganda techniques were not known before 1914. Kings, queens and national leaders have, throughout history, known the importance of rallying public spirits via the mass media of the day; from hiring town criers to paying press barons, to endowing playwrights with funding, they found numerous methods of projecting a supportive message to the wider public. The Bayeux tapestry, first commissioned in the eleventh century, is an early example of the art, colourfully weaving the story of William I vanquishing King Harold on the hillsides of Hastings to win the English throne for the Normans.

However, modern propagandists really learnt their stuff during WWI, with use of a whole palette of options: posters, postcards, advertising, caricature, photography, early film-making and newspaper stories. Here was Intro to Twentieth Century Propaganda Techniques 101; a fertile lecture series, full of practical tips, that others that came after would mine for ideas. In the first two decades of the century technological changes, such as high speed printing presses and early film, combined with enormous newspaper readership, were the fertile ground on which to plant the seeds of ideas and campaigns that had the potential to reach millions.

Kaiser Wilhlem II knew about the power of propaganda as our regular cartoonist and writer Martin Rowson outlines in his article. The Kaiser had the original idea for the 1896 cartoon Nations of Europe, with the plan of signing up European leaders to his campaign against the "yellow peril", the growing power of Japan. The Kaiser presented a copy of the sketch to his cousin the Tsar of Russia, perhaps he stuck one in the post to his other cousin Britain's George V too. Art's power to persuade was undeniable during the Great War. A century later Kitchener's poster with the thrusting finger demanding that "your country needs you" remains in the public consciousness in Britain, and its influence stretches further, continuing to spark copies and pastiches. Stereotypes, phrases, songs and ideas invented during this period have been resilient, and are remembered even 100 years later. So the idea of "packing up your troubles in your old kitbag" continues, the "Hun" of WWI cartoonists is still a reference, while the phrase "Spanish flu" continues to be used without many of us realising its root is in the censorship of WWI, when an influenza epidemic carried off millions →

Credit: C. and M. History Pictures / Alamy

ABOVE: A Soviet propaganda poster from 1975 celebrating the 40th anniversary of the launching of the Stakhanovite movement in 1935. The slogan reads "Use the traditions of the Stakhanovite movement!"

→ around the world. Spain was one of the few countries without media censorship in place when the epidemic struck and when it was reported on by the Spanish media, the flu consequently became "the Spanish flu".

The WWI global flu epidemic encapsulates both propaganda and censorship, and is an illuminating tale for all its manifestations. Many experts now believe the pandemic killed more than the war itself; at least 50 million across the world, more in a single year than the Black Death, as Alan Maryon-Davis charts in his fascinating article Into The Valley of Death. But when the first symptoms of this modern plague started to come to the attention of doctors and governments, large swathes of the world were at war. As young men tramped from all reaches and corners of their own countries to war zones, they were risking not only being hit in battle, but the chance of succumbing to the world's deadliest flu outbreak. With the world at war, governments were loathe to acknowledge the disease, and how many it was felling. It was feared the news of the deaths would undermine the war effort, and cause panic, if the full extent of the epidemic was acknowledged. Posters and newspaper advertising challenged the public with "Don't Let Flu Frighten You". Meanwhile, doctors struggled to identify what was causing the outbreak and how to tackle it. When censorship regulations finally began to relax, governments started to use propaganda methods of wartime to fight the medical battle. Public health posters with a simple message were placed in newspapers, to finally warn the public of the problem.

The tale of the WWI flu epidemic illustrates the great risk of cutting off the public from vital knowledge. But today things would be different. With our access to all sorts of social media, as well as the official outlets, it is unlikely that any government, or set of governments, could be able to keep a lid on news of a global disease sweeping through countries, leaving millions dead. The word would get out. In most parts of the world we have experienced an information revolution in the one hundred years since 1914; we are no longer in thrall to what governments deign to tell us; the question now is what and who to believe when we see it.

But plus ça change, plus c'est la même chose. As we approach the 1914 centenary the masters of the universe are still at it, trying to reach the public by swirling their magic. French cartoonist Plantu told one of our writers that he came under pressure from Nicolas Sarkozy to stop drawing him as a short man. Sadly, for Sarkozy that is, the whole thing backfired as every time he pushed Plantu, the artist's pen made the French big man smaller and smaller. And lately England's larger-than-life Education Secretary Michael Gove has been trying to bring the arts world into line with his line, writing of how culture has hijacked the reality of WWI with "left-wing" messages hidden in forms such as the television series Blackadder. Only an idiot would suggest that children be taught nothing but Blackadder; Mr Gove, no idiot he, is surely aware that it manages first to make people laugh, and then, in at least some children, to pique an interest in finding out what actually happened, in much the way that, say, Dumas or Walter Scott did as wildly best-selling historical novelists in the nineteenth century. Their novels were not always rigidly accurate, but so readable that at least some of what they wrote had an enthralled child asking: "What really happened here?" Fortunately, in increasingly non-deferential Britain, Mr Gove's anathema on a programme is likely only to increase interest watching it. For one thing has always been true – tell someone what they cannot read or watch or listen to, and they will sure as eggs is eggs reach for it the second you take your eyes off them. ☒

Rachael Jolley is editor of Index on Censorship

Credit: REX/Courtesy Everett Collection

ABOVE: A still from the film Fires Were Started, which was released in 1943, and was a propagandist documentary using footage of firemen during the Blitz

In this section

Days in the museums

43(1): 8/12 | DOI: 10.1177/0306422014521558

China keeps reinventing the way it tells its history and its role in World War II. Academic and author **Rana Mitter** reveals why

A MEMORIAL OPENED at the top of Songshan mountain in Linglong county in Yunnan province, southwest China, in September last year. The memorial consists of 402 statues of Chinese soldiers who fought the Japanese as part of an expeditionary force during WWII and has been established with the full backing of the Chinese Communist Party. But one element of the exhibit would be profoundly troubling to Chairman Mao, were he alive to see it. The soldiers who are being commemorated were not part of the Eighth Route or New Fourth Armies, the major communist forces during the conflict. They were part of the Nationalist army, the forces under Mao's old adversary, Chiang Kai-shek. Just a couple of decades ago, it would have been hard to imagine China's authoritarian communist government saying anything favourable about their deadly nationalist rivals whom they ultimately defeated in the civil war of 1946-49. Today, the nationalist war effort has become part of China's wider propaganda strategy against Japan. The story of this strange ideological reversal illustrates a wider point at the heart of China's struggle to project an idea of itself at home and in Asia today: Chinese propaganda about the meaning of World War II is becoming more, not less, important even as the conflict itself slips out of living memory. Interpretations of wartime history in China have profoundly significant consequences for the balance of power in the Asia-Pacific region in the years to come.

Anti-Japanese war propaganda is nothing new in China. In 1937, Japan's increasingly aggressive incursions into China led to war breaking out between the two nations. By the time the war ended in 1945, some 14 million or more Chinese had been killed, and 100 million had become refugees. During the eight years of war, propaganda was a staple of the Nationalists under Chiang Kai-shek and the Communists under Mao Zedong. Newspapers, cartoons, and adaptations of popular plays and operas all contributed to a growing sense of national resistance against invasion.

The war against Japan was quickly followed by a civil war, won by the Communists. During Mao's years in power, which included the frenzy of the Cultural Revolution, the Japanese continued to be the targets of official propaganda, turning up as foils in revolutionary Peking operas such as Legend of the Red Lantern. But overall, it was class warfare and the prospect of international anti-imperialist revolution that were the primary sources of ideological fuel under Mao. The war against Japan was reduced to a caricature in which the Chinese Communist Party had played the leading role, and no other Chinese or foreign actors had made any significant contribution.

ABOVE: Some 6,830 pairs of cloth shoes are laid on the ground at a square of the Nanjing Massacre Museum in Nanking to commemorate Chinese wartime forced labourers who died in Japan during World War II

Credit: Stringer/Reuters

However, in the 1980s, the Chinese Communist Party radically reinterpreted the meaning of the war in official propaganda. China's highest leaders decided that they would stress nationalism, not class warfare, as the binding ideological glue that would hold China together. Massive investment was placed in public education about the war, and three major museums were established as part of the change. In the northern city of Shenyang, a museum commemorated the Japanese invasion of Manchuria in 1931; the building is designed to resemble a desk calendar open at 18 September, the day of the invasion. In Nanjing, a museum was built on the site of one of the horrific massacres that marked the Japanese invasion of the city in December 1937. And in Beijing, a new museum opened commemorating the entirety of the war against Japan, defined initially as the eight years of full war between 1937 and 1945, but then extended, as has become commonplace within China itself, from 1931 to 1945 to include the invasion of Manchuria, and subsequent events.

There were many remarkable aspects of this decision. One was the fact that no →

ABOVE: Paramilitary policemen march during a memorial ceremony on the 82nd anniversary of Japan's invasion of China, at the September 18th History Museum in Shenyang, in September 2013

→ comprehensive museum of the wartime years had existed at all until that point. But the most notable change in emphasis was the way that the communist regime allowed a partial rehabilitation of their former deadly enemies: the nationalist regime that they had overthrown in the civil war of 1946-

The opening of previously hidden history has been partial and in service of a particular agenda

49. Through the Mao era, Chiang Kai-shek was a much more potent and real threat than the Japanese. Chiang was lurking in Taiwan, waiting to recapture the mainland. In contrast, while the Japanese did not recognize China diplomatically, they had extensive contact with China during much of the 1950s and 1960s; no such contacts existed with Taiwan. As late as the 1980s, it was still taboo to mention Chiang Kai-shek in anything but the most hostile terms.

In the past couple of decades, this situation has changed radically. Travel to Huangshan, for instance, just outside the southwestern city of Chongqing which served as China's wartime capital from 1937 to 1945. Huangshan was Chiang's retreat during the years of World War II, from where he saw the fires lighting up the skies of his capital as Japanese incendiary bombs repeatedly set it aflame. In Chiang's villa, which is preserved as a museum, you see accounts of Chiang's wartime resistance as a patriot who defended China against the invasion from that ultimate enemy, Japan. The ultimate manifestation of Chiang's rehabilitation is to be found at his birthplace in Xikou, in Zhejiang province. Walking around the town, you wouldn't know that Chiang had lost the civil war in 1949 – Chiang kitsch memorabilia can be found everywhere: fans, paperweights, and posters. His old home, which has been set up as yet another museum, is a masterpiece in

Credit: Stringer/Reuters

ideological contortion: in the photographic displays, Chiang is praised for his dedication to anti-Japanese resistance, but there is then a huge blank between 1945 and the late 1960s, when it is stated, rather lamely, that Chiang left for Taiwan (for reasons unnamed). The events illustrated only by an image of a rather benevolent looking Chiang and Madame Chiang, portrayed like any typical retired couple.

The city of Chongqing is one of the most important sites of this new official shaping of historical memory in China. During the era of Mao, it was impossible for the city to recall the moment that had made it a centre of not just Chinese but global attention for some eight years between 1937 and 1945. Any association with the wartime era was simply toxic because of the connections to the Nationalists. But in the past decade or two, the city has been making up for lost time. Chongqing party secretary Bo Xilai fell from power in 2012, but during his years in power he had made a point of allowing the city to stress its wartime history to raise its profile in the present day. Wartime sites such as embassies, or the house belonging to the American Commander-in-Chief of the China Theatre, General "Vinegar Joe" Stilwell, are now open as tourist attractions. War memorials and books commemorate the Nationalist dead as well as the Communist fallen.

The rehabilitation is not by any means complete. Most textbooks in high school will still tend to stress the communist contribution to winning the war over that of the nationalists. Also, there are huge areas of wartime history that still remain immensely hard to discuss. Collaboration with the Japanese is one of the most obvious ones of those. Wang Jingwei, the former Nationalist leader who defected to work with Japan in 1938, is still remembered as a traitor pure and simple, whose motivations deserve little analysis. There is no prospect of Wang Jingwei's old house being rehabilitated as a shrine.

The new understanding of the nationalist contribution has had some tangible and positive effects. In popular culture, there have been web projects and television programmes, such as the one hosted by popular Chinese television host Cui Weizhou, which have championed the cause of former nationalist soldiers. In 2013, remaining Nationalist veterans were finally given pensions by the state as a token of appreciation for their contribution to the anti-Japanese struggle.

However, the new emphasis on aspects of the Nationalist war effort does not mean a full and frank discussion about the war and its effects on China. The opening of previously hidden history has been partial and in service of a particular agenda: the reshaping of China's claims in Asia, particularly as they

Walking around the town, you wouldn't know that Chiang had lost the civil war in 1949

relate to Japan. After a period of relatively calm and cooperative interaction, the past five years or so has seen a heightening of tensions between China and Japan. There are multiple causes for this. Figures on Japan's right have made repeated claims that Tokyo's invasion and occupation of much of Asia in the 1930s and 1940s was a war of liberation, a view shared by none of Japan's neighbours. In addition, both countries are seeking a more assertive role in the Asia-Pacific region. But ultimately, China is much larger and sees itself as returning to its role as a regional hegemon. Also, Japan is, despite many flaws in its public sphere, ultimately a pluralist democracy. China is not, and the Chinese Communist Party has no intention of letting it become one. That means that the interpretation of the war in China in years to come is likely to fit in with an agenda that is shaped by the needs of the Party rather than by historians concerned to explore →

→ the historical facts. This includes the new warmth toward the nationalist war record.

In the past few months, the importance of the 1937-45 war against Japan in China's propaganda strategy has been raised significantly. When China declared its Air Defence Identification Zone (ADIZ) in November 2013 in an area that included the disputed islands, one of the most strongly assertive Chinese newspapers, the Global Times, declared that it was Japan that was the "prime target" of the move. The 70th anniversary of the 1943 Cairo Conference was also noted in Chinese news reporting because of the conference communiqué that declared that Japanese possessions in Asia would be returned after the war. This particular element of Chinese history is being used as a means of justifying present-day Chinese claims in the Pacific.

China has a good claim that it was the "forgotten ally" during World War II. In the West, we rarely remember the role that China played: while holding down some 750,000 or more Japanese troops, China suffered 14 million deaths with 100 million of its people becoming refugees. The United States used its huge sacrifices in the region as the basis for creating a regional role there that exists to the present day. But American hegemony comes ultimately through consensus. If Japan, Taiwan, South Korea, or the Philippines really wished to exclude US power from the region, they could do so. Yet China seems unable to calibrate its power in the region to achieve a similar effect, and its message about its wartime sacrifices has more resonance within China than it does externally. There is a very good case that without China's efforts in holding down the Japanese, Tokyo's empire in east Asia might have had a much longer life than it actually did. Yet the use of wartime history in China, even though it has reopened the story of the communists' former nationalist enemies, has yet to give China the propaganda boost that it so clearly hopes for. The story of the Yunnan veterans has finally been heard by their compatriots, but it has not yet managed to persuade the wider world that China has earned the right to greater power in today's Asia-Pacific. ☒

Rana Mitter is the author of China's War with Japan, 1937-45: The Struggle for Survival (Allen Lane), published in North America as Forgotten Ally: China's World War II. He is also professor of the History and Politics of Modern China, Institute for Chinese Studies, University of Oxford

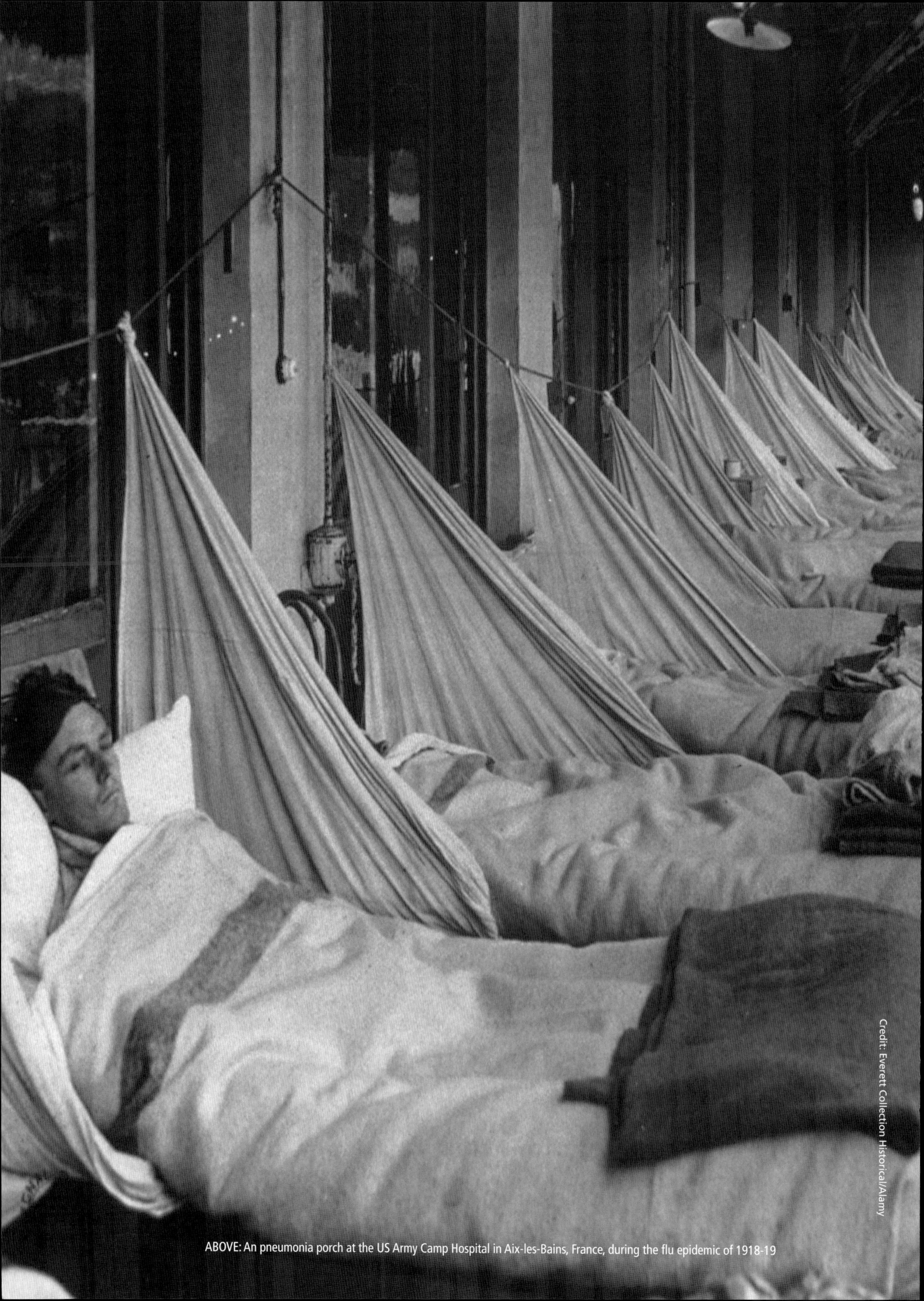

Credit: Everett Collection Historical/Alamy

ABOVE: An pneumonia porch at the US Army Camp Hospital in Aix-les-Bains, France, during the flu epidemic of 1918-19

Into the valley of death...

43(1): 14/20 | DOI: 10.1177/0306422013519544

The great influenza pandemic of 1918, at the end of World War I, killed at least 50 million people across the globe, despite huge efforts to contain and control it. But the first reaction of the Allied governments was to shroud it in a cloak of secrecy for fear of sapping morale and hindering troop movements just as the war was reaching a climax. **Alan Maryon-Davis** analyses what happened and wonders if it would be different today?

EVEN TODAY, WITH the cloak of secrecy long since lifted, no one knows exactly how or where it started. The great flu pandemic of 1918 was a global holocaust that seems to have arisen spontaneously among the shifting swathes of desperate, debilitated and chronically overcrowded humanity caught up in the maelstrom of World War I.

What we know for sure is that, in the summer and autumn of 1918 and the →

→ following spring, the pandemic swept without mercy through the fighting forces of the Western Front, the transit camps and supply routes, and the ports, towns and cities of neighbouring countries. Within a month or two it had reached almost every corner of the globe. We also know that it was the deadliest affliction ever visited upon humanity, killing at least 50 million people worldwide, probably nearer 100 million, several times more than 15-20 million killed by the war itself – and more in a single year than the Black Death killed in a century.

The pandemic came in three waves that merged into one another, differing greatly in severity. The preliminary phase was a scattered series of outbreaks of a prostrating respiratory illness variously called "three-day fever", "*la grippe*", epidemic bronchitis or "lung block". These outbreaks occurred in

One of the few countries where the press were free to publish news of the flu was Spain, so it was dubbed the "Spanish flu"

military camps as early as December 1916 at Étaples in France and Aldershot in England, culminating in a much more widespread contagion in spring 1918 among the rapidly massing US Army troops in dozens of huge training camps across the eastern United States.

As the American war machine built up its two-million-strong force, with many thousands of soldiers crossing the Atlantic every month, pouring into the ports, camps, billets and trenches of France and Flanders, the deadly disease came with them, spreading like wildfire. By early summer 1918 it was already hitting combatants and non-combatants alike in their hundreds of thousands throughout Europe, the US and beyond. India was particularly hard-hit, with as many as 17 million people dying, 5 per cent of the entire population.

Then, in early autumn 1918, just as the worst seemed to be over, a second, far more devastating, wave of influenza was unleashed on a world still reeling from the first onslaught. Somehow, no one knew why, the illness had become even more deadly than it had been in the summer. Case fatality rates had doubled or, in some communities, trebled – so that altogether about one person in every five of those infected perished.

The worst cases triggered bacterial pneumonia, which before the advent of antibiotics was almost invariably fatal. With a raging temperature and gasping for breath, patients appeared to be drowned by a massive accumulation of pus, fluid and blood in their lungs. Their fingers and lips turned blue and their complexion a pallid grey.

Everyone knew someone who had caught the deadly fever, but no one knew exactly what was causing it. Could it be influenza, which had been a regular visitor for centuries? Or was it a novel form of plague? Or perhaps some new typhus? Typical influenza was known to be especially dangerous for frail elderly people, infants and young children, and anyone with a serious medical condition. But this new disease was also devastating for previously healthy young adults who would normally shrug off ordinary influenza after a few days of misery. And unlike influenza, which typically struck in the winter months, this disease was happening in the summer and autumn. What could it be? Why didn't anyone say? Nobody in authority was even acknowledging its existence.

Most of Europe was subject to wartime censorship, as were belligerent allies overseas such as Australia, New Zealand, South Africa, Canada and the US, with stringent restrictions on what could be reported in newspapers and magazines or published in pamphlets, monographs and books. Blanket rules were applied to suppress key information for fear of providing the enemy with useful intelligence on the state of military readiness and capability, the resilience of the supply chain and morale on the home front. This meant that information on the real severity of the epidemic and details of the numbers and location of cases were not permitted.

One of the few countries where the press was free to publish news of the epidemic was neutral Spain. The unfettered Spanish papers had no hesitation in documenting the horrors and mounting death toll from the respiratory fever they loosely dubbed "influenza", relishing in particular the near-fatal illness of King Alfonso XIII. It didn't take long for word to spread that the ghastly new disease felling whole communities across the world must be the infamous "Spanish flu".

Some historians have asserted that, in Britain, the War Office was so anxious to conceal the true nature and extent of the disease that they deliberately leaned on the government to avoid giving practical information to the public on how best to protect themselves. Other commentators cite evidence to suggest that the real reason for the delay was rather more prosaic: during the first wave of the epidemic in early summer 1918 the Army Medical Services were still at a loss as to exactly what disease they were up against. Pathologists and epidemiologists in all the Allied nations were working round the clock to identify the causative agent and develop a vaccine, but there was no consensus as to which of several candidate bacteria it was. The possibility of a virus being to blame was hardly even considered, so little was known about viruses at the time.

As far as public information was concerned, Sir Arthur Newsholme, chief medical officer to Britain's public health body, the Local Government Board, refrained from issuing a notice to the civil authorities for the same reason: no one was certain of the diagnosis or what could be done about it.

Meanwhile, in the US, the authorities made similar attempts to hush things up and keep people in the dark regarding the true seriousness of the situation. No national official publicly acknowledged the real risks of the by-then-rampant epidemic. Instead an anxiety-provoking mix of truth, half-truth, distortion and downright lies was promulgated. As California senator Hiram Johnson remarked at the time: "The first casualty when war comes is truth." The US government's clumsy efforts to prop up national morale simply had the counter-effect of fostering fear.

The press echoed this misguided approach by making light of mortality figures and putting a positive spin on the horrendous struggle to save lives. According to historian John M Barry, day after day in hundreds of newspapers the reassurance rang out: "There →

ABOVE: Poster relating to the Spanish Flu epidemic in Chicago in late 1918 when censorship was being relaxed in some states

Credit: Everett Collection/REX

→ is no cause for alarm if precautions are observed."

At Camp Pike, near Little Rock, Arkansas, where 8,000 cases lined the corridors of the hospital over a peak four days and deaths were too many to list, the Arkansas Gazette blithely informed its readers: "Spanish influenza is plain *la grippe* – same old fever and chills."

Similarly, whilst hundreds of young conscripts were dying at Camp Dodge just outside Des Moines, Iowa, the city attorney was warning editors and journalists: "I would recommend that if anything is printed in regard to the disease it be confined to simple preventive measures – something constructive rather than destructive."

In Bronxville, New York, the local paper condemned "alarmism" and intoned that

By early summer 1918 it was already hitting combatants and non-combatants alike in their hundreds of thousands

"fear kills more than the disease and the weak and timid often succumb first". The Chicago Commissioner for Public Health, John Dill Robertson, proudly reported that nothing was done to interfere with the morale of the community: "It is our duty to keep the people from fear. Worry kills more people than the epidemic." All over the US, newspapers pushed out the same messages: "Don't Get Scared", "Don't Panic", "Don't Let Flu Frighten You to Death".

But not surprisingly the effect of all this reassurance was that people felt they were being kept in the dark. They could see their brothers and sisters, friends and neighbours succumbing to a mysterious and frightening disease, and they not only felt let down by their civic leaders but also all the more terrified of the unknown. The constant "Don't Get Scared" mantra was fomenting the very panic it was trying to subdue, and causing even more distress and disruption. It also hampered a coordinated civil response, which could have saved many lives.

By the time the armistice came in November 1918, the pandemic was at full spate and utterly unstoppable. Only then and in the months to follow, as censorship was relaxed, was the full horror of what had happened revealed to a world already stunned by four years of total war. And even then, demobilisation, with millions of troops returning home to their towns and villages, together with extreme shortages of food, shelter and medicines across war-torn Europe, meant the lethal pestilence persisted into the new year, with another, smaller, wave of misery and death in the spring of 1919.

Could anything like the great flu pandemic of 1918 happen again? And if so, could people again find themselves left largely in the dark?

There have been a number of viral pandemics since then. In the late 1950s we had "Asian flu", which came out of China and spread rapidly, hastened by air travel. Altogether it killed about two million people, particularly the frail elderly whose resistance was weak. Just over 10 years later a milder variant dubbed "Hong Kong flu", spread similarly across the globe.

In the early 1980s the world became aware of a mysterious auto-immune deficiency syndrome (AIDS) which had a predilection initially for gay men and intravenous drug users. The causative virus, HIV, was eventually isolated and its origins traced back via Haiti to west-central Africa. This pandemic is with us still.

In 2003 we saw the alarming outbreak of SARS (severe acute respiratory syndrome), a highly contagious and deadly form of viral pneumonia – again starting in Asia and quickly threatening to engulf the world via air travel. Only rapid action by the World Health Organization (WHO) and national public health authorities managed to contain its spread and prevent a global catastrophe.

And in 2009 the world braced itself for a pandemic of "swine flu", caused by influenza type A (H1N1), a near-copy of the 1918 virus similarly dangerous to previously healthy young adults. This flu originated in Mexico and rapidly spread to the US, Spain and elsewhere. This time, with early warning of the threat, the authorities were reasonably well prepared. They soon knew what organism they were up against and had some idea of how it might behave – although, as in 1918, no one really knew how severe it would be. Fortunately, the virus was nothing like as deadly as in 1918, and its fatalities were counted in the tens of thousands rather than tens of millions.

Over the past few decades the WHO and national public health services have set up a remarkably effective global surveillance and monitoring system, which can identify and track the progress of infectious diseases as they sweep across the globe. This system is authorised and supported by binding international agreements, with rapid reporting via the internet to health authorities and the mass media throughout the world. Within hours of a suspected human-to-human transmission being reported, its progress can be followed by anyone, anywhere.

This system relies on openness and transparency. Communicable diseases know no borders, and what happens on the other side of the world can all too rapidly overwhelm any nation's capacity to function. A shared responsibility for global health and wellbeing is recognised as essential. But the system has its vulnerabilities.

The first is at the very start of the alert chain – the response of the local health worker faced with a suspected case. Crucial decisions have to be made. Is there anything unusual or particularly worrying about this case? Should I report it to my superior? What samples do I need to take? How can I prevent it spreading to family, friends and neighbours? How quickly do I need to act? Will I get into trouble if I make a fuss? These first few hours are by far the weakest link in the chain, and the risks can only be minimised by proper training and backup. All countries need robust public health teams, especially in remote rural areas, with well-honed protocols and reliable lines of communication.

The next weak link is where disclosure of a virulent and dangerous disease by the authorities might have negative commercial or political consequences. In these circumstances there is obvious potential for coercion or corruption. It's a worrying prospect, and it would be comforting to think it wouldn't happen, but there have been many past instances when deception and delay in reporting outbreaks have cost lives.

A third vulnerability is similar to the cloak of secrecy that characterised the early weeks of the 1918 pandemic. How much should governments tell the people? How to strike the right balance between giving people the full facts and scaring the life out of them? One of the biggest worries the UK government had about the 2009 pandemic was that, in the worst-case scenario, people would be too frightened to leave their homes, essential services would break down and the economy would grind to a standstill. Detailed plans had been made for clearing hospitals and nursing homes to care for the sickest victims. Hundreds of refrigerated containers would have been commandeered to store the thousands of bodies awaiting burial. Volunteer forces were earmarked not only to keep essential services running but also to control panicky crowds and defend stockpiles of antivirals and antibiotics. This was scary stuff. How much did the public need to know?

In the event, there were almost daily bulletins and a balance was struck in terms of what was pushed out to the public and →

→ what was left unsaid. Fuller details were available on the net for those who wanted to know. There was no censorship, except where things touched on national security, but there was a selective approach to public communication: explicit about the risks and clear about the actions, but no more detail than was thought necessary. Subsequently, when the swine flu turned out to be much milder than feared, many people complained about too much hype causing too much anxiety.

The internet and social media have changed everything. For governments and individuals alike, secrets are much harder to keep. Even highly "secure" databases can be hacked and internal emails leaked. Not only are we now more aware of how much information governments are gathering about each of us, but also how much they are withholding from us. Increasingly, attempts at concealment fail. The political price of keeping the facts from the people is becoming ever more prohibitive.

So what can we expect with the next flu pandemic? We know it's not a question of if, but when. Pandemic flu remains a top priority for governments throughout the world. In June 2013 the World Health Organization issued revised pandemic influenza guidance, again emphasising that openness and transparency are key.

So too, however, is the "precautionary principle" of erring on the side of caution. Does that caution mean telling people more than they need to know, or withholding potentially "counterproductive" information from them? In the routine medical world the prevailing practice is to share everything with patients – all the risks, all the benefits – and help them decide a course of action. With a highly infectious pandemic the authorities have to exert much more command and control, particularly if things get so bad that a state of emergency is declared.

So will this mean a return to the cloak of secrecy when the next pandemic strikes? It will be interesting to see how closely history repeats itself. ☒

Alan Maryon-Davis is honorary professor in public health at King's College, London. He is a past president of the UK's Faculty of Public Health and a former director of public health in Southwark, London

Reel drama

43(1): 21/27 | DOI: 10.1177/0306422014523227

How were films were used as propaganda during World War II? We asked two writers for their views. **David Aaronovitch** argues that all's fair in war against fascist dictatorship, including seducing the United States into war with pretty faces and British accents. Then **Marc DiPaolo** takes a cinematic journey through the period's flicks and the messages they were selling

IN JUNE 1942 – at the recommendation of Winston Churchill – a Jewish Hungarian refugee, Alexander Korda, became the first film director to receive a knighthood. Korda had arrived in Britain 11 years earlier from Hollywood, set up a production company called London Films and constructed a film studio at Denham, just west of London. Over the next decade he became a stalwart of the British film business. However, it was not for services to that industry that Korda was cited, but for his "contribution to the war effort". So what services could a film producer-director render to the war effort?

Not by staying in Britain to face the Nazis, as the Hollywood stars Leslie Howard and David Niven did. In the early months of the war Korda was back in the United States and working on his movie The Thief of Baghdad, whose production had been shifted from Britain. But the anti-Nazi Korda could have returned home, as others did. Why, then, did he not?

Probably because he could be of far more use to his adopted country by staying in the US and becoming part of an effort to gain American support for Britain, than by going back to London. This had been the perception of the urbane ambassador to the United States, Lord Lothian. Appointed in the month that war broke out, Lothian advised the British government that it would be a good idea to maintain a substantial presence in Hollywood, producing films "with a strong British tone", which constituted "one of the best and subtlest forms of British propaganda".

The problem was relatively simple. The British government had always known that it required more time to be ready for a war against Germany. When Poland was invaded and war became unavoidable, Britain was under-armed and unprepared. The country needed as much help as it could get from the great democracy across the Atlantic.

But America, as measured by poll after poll and as enacted in a series of Neutrality Acts, wanted no repeat of 1917 and involvement in a European war. Though there was sympathy for Britain, even as the phoney war turned into the war for survival and Chamberlain was replaced by Churchill, there was a large bloc of American opinion that was resolutely opposed to any →

ABOVE: Vivien Leigh and Laurence Olivier in That Hamilton Woman (released as Lady Hamilton in the UK)

→ military assistance whatsoever for any of the belligerents. In the presidential election of November 1940, as London burned, Franklin Roosevelt – standing for his third term – felt compelled to promise his voters that no son of theirs would end up fighting in a foreign war. Churchill's elegant but desperate pleas even for surplus military equipment, such as old destroyers, were refused on the basis of public opposition.

Since no one in London could have predicted the attack on Pearl Harbor (let alone the subsequent German declaration of war on America), the working strategy was to draw the Americans into concrete acts of solidarity with their fellow democrats and Anglophones. And this strategy had a major role for someone like Korda.

In six weeks during the autumn of 1940, as the Battle of Britain was fought, Korda was at work shooting scenes for a film about the love affair between Emma Hamilton and Horatio Nelson. That Hamilton Woman, released in April 1941, starred Hollywood's hottest young couple, the Britons Vivien Leigh (fresh from Gone With The Wind), and Laurence Olivier.

As it happened the battle for American support was already being won, if slowly.

Credit: Moviestore Collection/REX

In March 1941, after votes in Congress, Roosevelt had signed the Lend Lease act, which "lent" old American ships and newer planes in return for leases on bases on British-owned territories. Nevertheless, the supposed role played by movies such That Hamilton Woman became the focus of anger on the part of those Americans campaigning against support for Britain. The America First Committee, the umbrella "stop the war" organisation that enjoyed mass support – particularly in the Midwest – condemned a Hollywood plot to persuade the US into fighting Germany. They called for a public boycott of propagandistic movies.

Some in Congress took the battle against British propaganda even further. The populist Republican senator from North Dakota, Gerald Nye, who had led an inquiry into American involvement in World War I, now announced that his committee would investigate the role of aliens in Hollywood in creating pro-war propaganda. In a foretaste of what was to come in the post-war era of the House Un-American Activities Committee, Nye summoned Korda to appear before him. The date set for the appearance was 12 December 1941. But by then such inquiries were academic.

Fifty years later the anti-war novelist Gore Vidal, in his book Screening History, recalled a movie-going adolescence "dominated.... by the seduction of the United States by England". With characteristic use of both the broad brush and the fine tip, Vidal discerned a modern parallel. "For those who find disagreeable today's Zionist propaganda," he wrote, "I can only say that gallant little Israel of today must have learned a lot from gallant little Englanders of the 1930s. The English kept up a propaganda barrage that was to permeate our entire culture.... Hollywood was subtly and not so subtly infiltrated by British propagandists."

Vidal believed the effort had started well before 1939. He saw it in the 1937 Elizabethan-era drama Fire Over England in which Flora Robson's Gloriana had seen off the foreign tyrant Philip of Spain. He even noted that there was nothing filmic filling the historical gap between The Prince and the Pauper (which depicts the future Edward VI) and the reign of Elizabeth adding, either bizarrely or in self-mockery, "I now realize that British Intelligence had kept from us the poignant shortness of Edward VI's reign in order to build up his half-sister, Elizabeth".

This sin of Anglophile commission was made worse by the neglect of America's own history. Until Gone With The Wind, wrote Vidal, American movie-goers "served neither Lincoln nor Jefferson Davis; we served the Crown". Vidal was a young supporter of America First and never recanted his anti-war views. And we can see how, in retrospect, he wrote up his own history to support his defeated views.

Churchill's elegant but desperate pleas even for surplus military equipment, such as old destroyers, were refused on the basis of public opposition

In fact, 1939 and 1940 saw two major movies about Abraham Lincoln, including one starring Henry Fonda. The same years brought box office success to two epics of American history, Drums Along the Mohawk and Northwest Passage. And there were, in the late 1930s, dozens of Hollywood period films based on Russian and French history.

Viewed today, Korda's That Hamilton Woman is nine parts romance to one part message. It's quite likely that most of its US fans missed the Hitler-Napoleon association. In fact the greatest propaganda value of the film is probably its existence: →

→ English-speaking popular British actors depicting scenes involving Britain.

Indeed it was a perception from the earliest days of the war that British propaganda in the US should look as little like propaganda as possible, for fear of alienating its audience and strengthening isolationism. One example of effective propagandistic filmmaking was the short documentary London Can Take It, shown in thousands of US cinemas during the Blitz.

The commentary was read in sober, restrained tones, by Quentin Reynolds - an American newspaper correspondent based in London. "I am a neutral reporter," said Reynolds, "I have seen Londoners live and die....." But there are no pictures of bodies or of weeping relatives, just of people going about their lives in a city that is being bombed. Sometimes with humour. For example, the shops are open. In fact, says Reynolds, "many of them are more open than usual". Over one scene of Londoners in a street Reynolds says of the German bombers, "they'll be over tonight. They'll destroy a few buildings and kill a few people. Probably some of the people you're looking at now".

In the battle for freedom... and against fascist dictatorship, it seemed an odd scruple not to use your very best arguments in every situation

This, if anything, is propaganda by understatement. Though American viewers did not know it, the film was made and written by a team belonging to the legendary documentarist Humphrey Jennings under the auspices of the Ministry of Information. Reynolds voice-over was recorded, in the words of the American historian Stephen Budiansky, "in the bar of London's posh Savoy Hotel – from which Reynolds rarely ventured forth during the day, and from whose basement air-raid shelter he never ventured forth at night".

Strangely, though, that is the only aspect of the film that is misleading. The story told to the Americans was actually the same story Britons were telling themselves. In fact it's the same story we still tell. A story that – more or less – was true. As the best propaganda is.

Gore Vidal, and many other Americans who opposed military aid to Britain and American involvement in a European war, viewed anything that could be seen as propaganda as being essentially illegitimate. It was a lie dressed as the truth. It was something done to one set of people by another with the idea of altering or strengthening their views. Warmongers and British agents were intent on putting American lives in jeopardy and were unscrupulous about how they procured their objective.

To almost any British person of a certain age these objections seem almost beside the point. In the battle for freedom (and for Britain by 1940 it was certainly that) and against fascist dictatorship, it seemed an odd scruple not to use your very best arguments in every situation you could, to assist in national salvation. What, in this situation, was propaganda but a form of advertising in which the stakes were stratospherically higher than boosting sales of a motor car or a soap powder? Standing where I stand (and might easily never have existed to stand), it is hard to escape the conclusion that sometimes propaganda is a very good thing. X

David Aaronovitch is an author and journalist and tweets @daaronovitch. He is chair of Index on Censorship

Tools of war

Films with a propaganda message were an important part of the Allies' attempt to bring the United States into World War II. ***Marc DiPaolo*** *takes a look at cinema history, films, their message and impact*

"You cannot make peace with dictators!" cries Lord Nelson. "You have to destroy them! Wipe them out!" In this dialogue from the 1941 film Lady Hamilton, the cinematic Nelson is calling for Napoleon's blood but the actor playing him, Laurence Olivier, is breaking the fourth wall, directly addressing a pre-Pearl Harbor American moviegoing audience and (c)overtly calling for military support in the war against Hitler's Germany.

Throughout the film, Nelson educates his lover (Vivien Leigh in the title role) about the need to defeat Britain's enemies. Lady Hamilton, in turn, provides Nelson the love and support he requires to fortify him for battle. Essentially, Hamilton is to Nelson what Ilsa Lund would later be to Victor Laszlo in Casablanca (1942): "part of his work, the thing that keeps him going". Without Ilsa's love, Victor would fall and the Nazis would conquer the free world; without Lady Hamilton's love, Nelson would have lacked the will to defeat Napoleon at sea. In this respect, Leigh's Hamilton is one of several cinematic heroines of World War II-era films who symbolically represented a bold-but-embattled Mother England fighting a gendered, nationalistic conflict against the German Fatherland.

Released in the United States under the name That Hamilton Woman, Lady Hamilton was one of several anti-Nazi propaganda films made by expatriate British filmmakers in America who were both officially, and unofficially, working with Winston Churchill to coax the US into joining the Allies. Much like the 1940 Olivier and Greer Garson adaptation of Pride and Prejudice that preceded it, Lady Hamilton was a "heritage" film romance produced during the early years of the war featuring a heroine who exemplified the best qualities of British society. When conceiving of these projects, Churchill and his filmmaker collaborators calculated that the glamour and charisma of British actresses such as Garson and Leigh would challenge American perceptions of Great Britain as an aristocratic, outmoded, and snobbish society, and convince those living in the Colonies that British culture must endure.

In some respects, an infamous English courtesan made an unlikely choice for a character simultaneously representing Mother England and the best of British culture, but this was a sanitised version of Lady Hamilton appearing on screen. According to Molly Haskell, who wrote an essay on the film in 2009 for The Criterion Collection, producer-director Alexander Korda expressed some concern that the well-spoken and poised Leigh was not "vulgar" enough in the title role, but she chided him: "My dear Alex, you wouldn't have given me a contract if I was vulgar." Olivier, for his part, felt constrained playing Nelson as an iconic hero destined for glorious victory and death at Trafalgar instead of as a complex, flawed human being. Those who viewed the film after it was complete had different reservations. Hays Code-era censors and religious filmgoers of the time had some scruples about a movie that placed a romantic gloss on both the historically adulterous relationship between Nelson and Hamilton and on the contemporary adulterous affair between their actor counterparts, Olivier and Leigh.

Nevertheless, the film was effective as both a screen romance and as war propaganda. Churchill himself claimed Lady Hamilton as his favourite film, saw it more than 80 times, and carried a copy of the print with him whenever he travelled. Perhaps he was proud of the role he played in its production. According to film historian Stacey Olster, it was Churchill who asked Korda to make a movie about the romance between Hamilton and Nelson that would "promote Britain's historic role as a scourge of tyrants". And, as the Internet Movie Database attests, Churchill ghost-wrote the Nelson speech and other monologues with similarly anachronistic political significance. This claim is consistent with British film historian Amy Sargeant's observation that Churchill was sometimes directly involved with the creative output of the British film industry during his tenure as both minister of defence and prime minister of the wartime coalition government.

But not everyone was as enamored with Lady Hamilton as Churchill was. Pacifistic and isolationist groups in America boycotted the film, and the Senate Foreign Relations Committee accused Korda of operating a British espionage and propaganda centre on American soil, Olster wrote. Notably, the 7 December 1941 attack on Pearl Harbor may have saved Korda from prosecution. He returned to Britain and a knighthood in 1942 in recognition for his contribution to the war effort.

Korda's knighthood is unsurprising in light of the high regard both the Axis and Allies held the film medium as a means of spreading their ideologies domestically and abroad. As Philip Taylor, author of Munitions of the Mind: A History of Propaganda (1990) writes, "The Second World War witnessed the greatest propaganda battle in the history of warfare. For six years, all the participants employed propaganda on a scale that dwarfed all other conflicts… [T]he continued →

→ development of the communications revolution had, since the advent of sound cinema and radio, provided a direct link between those they governed, and between the government of one nation and the people of another. Propaganda was in this respect the alternative to diplomacy."

Indeed, World War II itself was a "cinematic war", as John Whiteclay Chambers II and David Culbert wrote in World War II: Film and History. "From the outset, governments and national motion-picture industries used moving images – newsreels, documentaries, and feature films – to help mobilise populations for war.... Motion pictures provided an effective means of building unity in World War II in part because audiences in urban, industrialised nations, such as the United States, had been accustomed in the preceding decades to going to movie theatres regularly as a way of obtaining information and entertainment."

The gorgeous, virtuous British women of the cinema were not merely the bait to lure reluctant Americans to the frontlines in the manner described above. These regally beautiful and morally upright women were also the means of comforting the people of Britain in times of trial – especially during the Blitz. In Fires Were Started in 1943, documentary-style images of the Queen surveying the devastation in the wake of the German bombing of civilian populations were meant to have a cathartic effect on domestic viewers. Outside of the realm of cinema, the writings of Regency-period novelist Jane Austen had a similarly calming effect on the people of Britain, and sales of her novels tripled during the war. Pride and Prejudice was a source of comfort to Churchill during a period when he was confined to bed with illness. However, he did marvel that Austen was able to write stories that appeared to be free of emotionally fraught references to the French Revolution and Napoleonic wars. "What calm lives they had," he observed.

Both the book and the film versions of Pride and Prejudice were fixtures of pro-British World War II propaganda. As Robert Lawson-Peebles observes in European Conflict and Hollywood's Reconstruction of English Fiction, the 1940 adaptation of Pride and Prejudice was part of the same propaganda project as Lady Hamilton. It was a literary adaptation, but it was, first and foremost, a war film designed to cure Americans of their troubling tendency to dislike stuffy Brits. According to Lawson-Peebles, Austen's novel is about the limitations that social class, economics, and strict gender roles placed upon women living in nineteenth century England, but the film adaptation is utterly unconcerned with such matters. Instead, Greer Garson's Elizabeth Bennett is involved in a project of democratising Olivier's Mr Darcy, making him less class-conscious and snobbish and more palatable to American audiences. Essentially, the Darcy rehabilitated by Lizzie seen at the end of the film is much more worth saving from the Nazis than the one at the start of the film, and that is what the film is really about.

Since the goal of the movie is to make the British aristocracy less offensive to American sensibilities, one of the central antagonists of the novel, Lady Catherine de Bourgh, is transformed from villain into hero in the final reel. In Austen's novel, de Bourgh opposes the union between Darcy and Elizabeth because Darcy would be marrying beneath his station into the scandal-ridden Bennett family and because she wants Darcy to marry her own daughter, Anne. In the film, de Bourgh is secretly in favor of the Darcy-Bennett union and is working with Darcy behind the scenes to secure Elizabeth's hand. By refashioning de Bourgh into a benign figure, the film essentially robs Elizabeth of her victory over de Bourgh and considerably undercuts Elizabeth's heroism and gravitas. However, fidelity to the novel was of less significance to the production team than aiding the war effort, so this major alteration was made to the narrative for practical and propagandistic purposes, much to the chagrin of literary scholars and devotees of the novel. Sadly, the film's cartoonish renderings of Austen's oeuvre as pro-aristocracy, broadly comic, and Cinderella-style fairy-take romance devoid of any feminist or intelligent satirical content continue to distort reader perceptions of her books, making them seem trivial, escapist fare in the eyes of far too many.

While some American pacifists were suspicious of British and American co-productions such as Pride and Prejudice – and for good reason – Hollywood grew gradually more bold in its support of the British side of the war as war fever grew in America. In fact, the American Office of War Information eventually began encouraging American filmmakers to join exiled British directors such as Korda in making British heritage films. Instead of a British filmmaker living abroad, an American director, William Wyler, would be the one chosen to helm Mrs. Miniver (1942), a film based on a 1939 British book that had found enormous popularity in the US. Jan Struther's bestseller began life in 1937 as a series of lighthearted, semi-autobiographical columns in The Times of London. Following the invasion of Poland, the column transformed into a chronicle of how the horrors of World War II changed the lives of an average British housewife and her family living in a village just outside of London. Americans read in suspense, as Mrs. Miniver felt compelled to secure gas masks for her family, marvelling how the once safe British family home could come under such threat from foreign attack. Eager to cast a popular actress to play the beloved title heroine, Wyler chose Garson.

Film studies commentator Meredith Hicks describes the film's plot and propagandistic project in her essay, Greer Garson and the Good

War: How We All Learned to Stop Worrying and Love the Great Lady:

> Kay Miniver is first introduced agonizing over whether or not she should buy a hat that she desperately wants, afraid that she cannot afford it. She decides to anyway and is ecstatic. Beginning with this image sets up the transition from self-involved Kay Miniver of rosy pre-war England to the stronger Mrs. Miniver of the title who shows her true mettle in the way she handles air raids and a downed Nazi pilot in the domestic, feminized space of her own kitchen. The central symbol of the Miniver rose stems from the pre-war practice of flower shows that go on despite the threat of air raid, binding the ideas of consumerism and pre-war simplicity with what they were fighting for.

While Garson is the centerpiece of the narrative, audience sympathy is also evoked by her son, who enlists in the Royal Air Force, her beautiful daughter-in-law, who is killed by the German forces during an attack on her village, and by her husband, who aids in the Dunkirk evacuation. The finale concerns a sermon by the village vicar, who explains that civilian casualties call for civilian participation in the war effort. As the vicar declares: "This is the People's War. It is our war. We are the fighters. Fight it then. Fight it with all that is in us. And may God defend the right."

The two centrepiece scenes were written and rewritten, shot and reshot to make sure they achieved their maximum dramatic effect – and were the most powerful possible war propaganda. The segment in which Mrs. Miniver is held hostage in her kitchen by a German soldier was first filmed before Pearl Harbor, and – in that version of the segment – she was allowed to show fear and the German a modicum of humanity. After Pearl Harbor, the segment was reshot, and Garson boldly smacks the soldier in the face and overpowers him after he evilly boasts that the Third Reich will destroy all that she cares for. In a similar vein, Wyler and the actor playing the vicar, Henry Wilcoxon, collaborated on the vicar's speech the night before it was filmed, rewriting it and refining it until they were sure it was ready for the camera. The result was a propaganda speech so powerful that Roosevelt had it reprinted on millions of pamphlets and flown and dropped over occupied Europe.

Mrs. Miniver was an American attempt at adapting a British novel and it wasn't entirely successful from the British perspective. Several London film critics mocked the movie as being a mawkish and juvenile American attempt at voicing solidarity in a global conflict that they didn't understand in the slightest. In contrast, Joseph Goebbels cited the film as an admirable template for German propaganda efforts, while Churchill declared Mrs. Miniver "more powerful than a fleet of battleships." Even more than Goebbels' positive assessment of Mrs. Miniver, Churchill's justifiably famous remark is a striking testimony to the power of cinematic narrative as a weapon of war.

To a degree, none of the films discussed in this article have stood the test of time. Lady Hamilton, Pride and Prejudice, and Mrs. Miniver are all remembered, studied, and occasionally watched, but few modern-day viewers would join Churchill in claiming any of them as a favourite film, despite the enduring appeal of Garson and Leigh as silver screen stars. The underlying propagandistic purposes of the films are too readily apparent, making all of them, to a degree, as melodramatic and silly as the British newspaper critics felt Mrs. Miniver was. The seams in the films are particularly obvious during peacetime viewings, though all three films might seem somewhat less absurd when watched during a time of modern-day conflict. In some respects, the propaganda-saturated news and films that have been produced during the protracted "war on terror" – with their over-the-top, bloody computer graphics and Holst-style war music soundtracks – are even less subtle, sophisticated, and artistically worthwhile than these three films are.

Still, melodramatic and omnipresent war propaganda – new and old – reminds us that a war film need not necessarily be subtle (or be good art) to be effective as a means of calling the public to arms. We can pretend we are too smart to be taken in by hawks shedding crocodile tears during overwrought speeches punctuated by the flourishing of trumpets, but those tears and those trumpets are sometimes too insistent to block out completely. And how much easier it is for propagandists to whip us all up into a bloodthirsty frenzy when the spokesperson for the war effort – the one uttering the rallying cry – is a beautiful woman? What if it is the best and most beautiful woman your country has ever seen the like of? Can her call to arms be ignored? This is a sobering, frightening question to contemplate, even if the woman is on "our" side, and even if there are real reasons to fear and fight "the enemy."

As historian Anne McClintock observes, "All nationalisms are gendered, all are invented, and all are dangerous." ☒

Marc DiPaolo is assistant professor of English and film at Oklahoma City University. He wrote War, Politics and Superheroes and Emma Adapted: Jane Austen's Heroine from Book to Film. He is co-editor (with Bryan Cardinale-Powell) of Devised and Directed by Mike Leigh

It's all Greek...

43(1): 28/33 | DOI: 10.1177/0306422014522185

Christos Syllas interviews historians about how propaganda was used by all sides in the Greek civil war and its implications

EVEN TODAY, ECHOES of the propaganda used during the civil war in Greece in the 1940s are influencing the current political turmoil in Athens. The dividing lines between communists and the Greek government were so sharply drawn that they have never really disappeared from the social and political consciousness.

The outbreak of the civil war in Greece in 1946 and the propaganda used by both sides during the struggle cannot be properly understood without realising that Greece was then on the frontline of the developing Cold War.

The United States was worried about Soviet expansion outside eastern Europe and into the Mediterranean area, so the Greek Communist Party and its military wing the Democratic Army of Greece (DSE) were considered a real danger.

Britain, which had carried the economic and political burden of supporting the Greek government against the communists was now concentrating on rebuilding itself after the war, so it was left to the US to undertake the role of strengthening the Greek National Army, under the the Marshall Plan.

As violence escalated after 1947, distrust was the main ingredient of communicating any political message. As thousands of prosecutions, executions, and violent relocations took place, propaganda in the civil war did not leave any room for reconciliation or even second thoughts.

The government side hunted down communists for "delivering" the country to its "northern neighbours", Slav-Macedonians and Bulgarians, while the DSE said the regime was a "monarcho-fascist army" which was fighting for "an unjust cause for the American dollar men".

Giorgos Margaritis, professor of modern history at Aristotle University of Thessaloniki, told Index: "The government side always declared that a bigger Greece including the Balkans area was desirable. The fact that the National Liberation Front and the Greek People's Liberation Army (EAM and ELAS), and later on the DSE, were supported by Slav-Macedonians and by the communist states of Yugoslavia, Bulgaria and Albania, was a reason for national treason. Nationalists and right-wingers considered communists as non-patriots, as national traitors."

Polymeris Voglis, assistant professor of modern history at the University of Thessaly added: "The government propaganda emphasised the treacherous character of the communists who aimed for Greece's partition. Above all though, it did not recognise communists as political adversaries. The regime was always attributing to them characteristics of criminals. Political prisoners, for example, were never acknowledged as such, and they were registered as common law criminals.

→

22

→ "In much the same spirit, the DSE denied for a long period that a civil war was being fought. It claimed that it was a national liberation struggle against the British and the Americans. It was like a second resistance after the Nazis".

Even though the illiteracy rates at the time of the war were reasonably high, newspapers, brochures and print material were used widely for propaganda purposes.

Professor Voglis said: "From 1945 there were repeated government attacks on communist newspapers and printing offices. However, during the civil war the Greek Communist Party (KKE) managed to build a strong network of newspapers and other print material. Apart from the official newspaper of the KKE, The Radical (*Rizospastis*), which was banned in 1947, there were 10 illegal newspapers and magazines distributed in the areas controlled by the DSE during 1948 and 1949. Communist printing presses became busier as the war escalated. In 1947, between 36 and 39 titles were published by the Greek Communist Party, publications such as instructions for guerilla warfare, short novels and political speeches. In 1949, the number of such books and pamphlets increased to 220."

By 1949, however, official military censorship was imposed upon any news about the civil war

On the other hand, the government controlled the bourgeois press, including the right-wing and conservative newspapers as well as those with a more liberal centrist orientation. Tasos Kostopoulos, a member of the prominent Greek investigative journalistic team Ios, and an experienced writer on civil war issues, said: "The bourgeois press at the time was perfectly aligned with government interests. In 1946, the Macedonian Comitat, a secret organisation, was used as a mechanism to execute armed communists, and was backed by the managers of three right-wing newspapers Estia, Embros, and Elliniko Aima. It was also used to keep the King-in-exile George II informed, while financing anti-communist units, from the money of local capitalists."

The polarisation created by the war struggle meant communists were depicted as violent gangsters by the right-wing and conservative press.

Prokopis Papastratis, professor emeritus of modern Greek history at Panteion University of Athens, told Index: "The articles in these newspapers presented the communist guerilla fighters as 'dirty', 'bloodthirsty', 'bandits', 'mobsters', and 'terrorists'. Sometimes there were pictures of hostages and dead fighters with the use of the above stereotypes. Women were also presented in a morally dubious way, as sexual objects being exploited by the leadership of DSE."

Buying a newspaper at the time was quite costly, and newspapers were dependent on a poor railway infrastructure for distribution, so radio had a stronger influence on people. It was instant and not dependent on literacy. Radio had already been used for propaganda purposes during the occupation a few years before: the first radio broadcast in Athens took place in 1938, during the Metaxas' dictatorship (1936-41) and under the auspices of the puppet government which ruled occupied Greece from 1941 until the end of the war.

George Pleios, professor at the department of communication and media studies, National and Kapodistrian University of Athens, gave Index a detailed analysis of the role radio played in civil war propaganda.

"From the government side in 1948 there was the Athens radio station as well as the armed forces radio station. On the other hand, DSE's radio station was Free Greek Radio (Eleftheri Ellada)," said Professor Pleios.

He went on to explain the content of the broadcasts and the discourses that were produced. "From 1946 onwards, the Athens radio station stopped broadcasts for the British forces and launched new ones for the American forces. The armed forces radio station had a popular entertainment programme with a very small news section. The government's broadcasts were characterised by anti-communist propaganda where DSE fighters were portrayed as 'mobsters' and as 'agents of the enemies' who conspired to obtain part of the Greek territory. On the other hand, Free Greek Radio was totally under the control of DSE. Some of its broadcasts were entertainment programmes designed to boost the morale of the guerilla forces. Interestingly, the broadcasters read articles from the government-controlled press and they would comment on them. At the heart of their propaganda remained the government dependency on the British or the Americans: most of the time they could not escape simplifications in building an unprecedented anti-Americanism. Also, their discourse included references to a class struggle: they spoke of a war motivated by plutocracy."

At the time, several commercial films were censored because the government suspected they negatively depicted the Greek army. However, the DSE managed to use its own visual material for internal propaganda.

Professor Margaritis said: "There was a special agency within the DSE. There was an organised film crew that showed speeches and pictures from the guerilla forces. Because of the constant relocation, internal propaganda was carried out at places that had already been 'captured'. Bear in mind that every piece of propaganda material, such as newspapers, and pamphlets were strictly forbidden."

As the war escalated in 1948, news appeared only in the back pages of the bourgeois press. The newspapers in Athens underreported the conflicts and consequently undermined the war which was mainly fought in the periphery. By 1949 however,

ABOVE: A Greek commando during the Greek civil war as captured on the front cover of Picture Post

Credit: Bert Hardy/ Picture Post/ IPC Magazines/ Getty Images

official military censorship was imposed upon any news about the civil war.

Professor Voglis said: "From 1948 onwards, the country was in a 'state of siege'. Civil war news was systematically underreported and, following a huge wave of violence, officially censored in 1949. If someone read newspapers like Vima, Kathimerini or Acropolis, he wouldn't properly understand that a civil war was going on. However, we should note that DSE forces never really captured any big city. It only controlled remote and mountain areas."

In order to fully understand the limits of political expression at the time a legal perspective can be very useful. Christos Papastylianou, associate professor of law at the University of Nicosia explained that there was a continuity in legislating before and →

→ during the civil war; a continuity that suggests the political intentions of those in power.

"On July 1945, the emergency law 453 on hunting down bandits essentially identified common law criminals with communists. In the history of law, 453 is a foreshadowing of what lay ahead. One year later, on May 1946, the government issued a decree authorising administrative deportation without judicial decision. Any person suspected of acting against social order or national security was punished by exile. The emergency law 509/1947 seemed to complete the sequence by forbidding one political party, the Greek Communist Party for the first time in history. It gave the green light to the government to arrest, execute and hunt down those fighting for the DSE and their sympathisers."

Indicative of the government strategy combined with the use of legislative power was the fact that even after the end of civil war and the defeat of the communists, the government insisted on propagating "national unity" and punished and tried to re-educate anyone (dissidents, communists) who failed the "patriotism" test.

Professor Papastylianou explained: "The island called Makronisos which was used as a place of imprisonment for dissidents, was created on a legal basis. The aim was to 'educate' its inmates to become nationalists."

Approaches to the civil war's historiography vary, according to political inclinations and access to sources. The main propaganda pattern around "the nation" and all the consequent recriminations however continue today. The rhetoric of the current right-wing government and the neo-fascist Golden Dawn as well as of Syriza's opposition party, reflect the old political contradictions. It can also be observed in the political discourse of non-parliamentary political groups, anti-authoritarian collectives and anarchists.

"The left says that the military part of the civil war ended in 1950," said Professor Pleios, referring to the non-stop political persecutions against the left, until the end of the military junta period in 1974.

"However, I think that the political substance of what was at stake during the conflict never came up. To an extent, no side managed to clearly explain its social and economic model for the future. There were probably two conflicting models: the bourgeois democracy and liberal economy model, essentially capitalism, and the Soviet model representing communism. However, what finally prevailed was a war climate with accusations of national treason."

Professor Margaritis agreed, offering his explanation from a class-struggle point of view: "In reality there were two production models conflicting at the time. The one that could be based upon farmers, proletarians and other working class people and the other based on a 'local' capitalism model built upon international subsidies. The second model prevailed. While guerilla forces were winning in the countryside, the Marshall Plan subsidies helped the supremacy of the national army while building urban economies. Local elites profited out of the war. A middle-class was under formation while proletarians were being squeezed in the cities and in the countryside. Constant relocations meant many of them often found themselves working for nothing."

Propaganda techniques and patterns were used according to the capacity of the conflicting sides and the means available to them.

The supremacy of the government was obvious. It was supported by the mainstream press and used a strong army to attack the communists' infrastructure.

As a way of intimidating and incriminating the enemy, propaganda was used intensively on both sides to present what they saw as the "real danger", but propaganda was also based on the real struggle between nationalists and the dissidents, namely communists.

A legal framework was set up that allowed the Greek state and the larger right-wing to suppress communist supporters, to put them in exile, and consequently built the narrative of being the civil war winners.

From a moralist's point of view, one can find truth in the discourses and the arguments produced. Judging by what political activists say today, the rhetoric used now carries on the old divisions: nationalists versus dissidents, capitalists versus workers, elites versus the poor. It is as if those old propaganda dividing lines never ceased to exist.

A major challenge, for all of us, is to see beyond the rhetoric and understand the intentions of political adversaries.

Christos Syllas is a freelance journalist based in Athens, Greece

COLLAGE

COLLAGE CAPTION 1: Top left, One exhausted guerrilla fighter surrenders to the Greek army during the Greek civil war
Credit: Bert Hardy/ Picture Post/ Getty Images

COLLAGE CAPTION 2: Top right, Refugee children in a filthy cellar at Piraeus during the Greek civil war
Credit: Haywood Magee/Picture Post/Getty Images

COLLAGE CAPTION 3: Bottom, A truck carries a band of government soldiers along a rocky mountain pass during the Greek civil war
Credit: Bert Hardy/ Picture Post/ Getty Images

Drawing out the dark side

43(1): 34/40 | DOI: 10.1177/0306422014524519

When it comes to depicting war, humour can be a critic's most dangerous weapon, says **Martin Rowson**, as he trips through the history of cartoons

AS A POLITICAL cartoonist, whenever I'm criticised for my work being unrelentingly negative, I usually point my accusers towards several eternal truths.

One is that cartoons, along with all other jokes, are by their nature knocking copy. It's the negativity that makes them funny, because, at the heart of things, funny is how we cope with the bad – or negative – stuff.

Whether it's laughing at shit, death or the misfortunes of others, without this hard-wired evolutionary survival mechanism that allows us to laugh at the awfulness running in parallel with being both alive and human, apes with brains the size of ours would go insane with existential terror as soon as the full implications of existence sink in. Which, for most people, would be when you're around three years old.

And if that doesn't persuade them, I usually then try to describe that indescribable but palpable transubstantiation that occurs when you shift from the negative to the positive, and a cartoon sinks from being satire to becoming propaganda.

Though here, of course, I'm not being entirely honest, because in many ways cartoons are propaganda in its purest form. This is because the methodology of the political cartoon has most in common with the practices of sympathetic magic and, likewise, its purposes are invariably malevolent.

Indeed, I've often described caricature in particular and political cartooning more generally as a type of voodoo, doing damage at a distance with a sharp object, in this case (usually) a pen.

Certainly the business of caricature is a kind of shamanist shape-shifting, distorting the appearance of the victim in order to bring them under the control of the cartoonist and subjecting them thereafter to ridicule or opprobrium. In short, political cartoons should truly be classified not as comedy but as visual taunts. And taunts, of course, have been an integral ingredient of warfare for millennia.

Within the twisted plaiting of taunts, posturing and brinkmanship that ultimately ended in the hecatombs of the Western Front in World War I you can just about tease out one thread trailing back to a cartoon.

The original sketch for the allegorical 1896 cartoon Nations of Europe: Join in Defence of Your Faith! was by Kaiser Wilhelm II of Germany, though he left the job of the finished artwork to professionals. Its purpose was to stiffen the resolve of

European leaders against the "yellow peril" coming from east Asia, and to this end the Kaiser presented a copy of the cartoon to his cousin Tsar Nicholas II of Russia.

It's generally agreed that the cartoon played a small but significant part in influencing the Tsar's confrontational policy towards Japan, which ended in Russia's humiliating defeat in the 1904-05 Russo-Japanese war.

The subsequent revolutions, regional wars and growing European instability erupted nine years later with the general mobilisation of the Great Powers, and the cartoonists were mobilised along with everyone else.

Although a perennial taunt against the Germans is that they have no sense of humour, they had as rich a tradition of visual satire as anyone else. In the pages of both Punch and the German satirical paper Simplicissimus, the enemy was caricatured identically as alternatively preposterous and terrifying. Both sides showed the other in league with skeletal personifications of Death, or transformed into fat clowns, foul or dangerous animals or, in British cartoons about Germans, as sausages.

There were also scores of cartoons showing German soldiers bayoneting Belgian babies in portrayals of "The Beastly Hun" and, later, cartoons showing the Germans harvesting the corpses of slain soldiers for fats to advance their war effort.

All sides taunted each other by attacking their nations' supposed leaders, using the caricaturist's typical tools. Thus the Kaiser, mostly thanks to his waxed moustache, acted as a synecdoche for Germany's defining perfidy. In one cartoon from 1915, when Britain's George V stripped his cousin, the Kaiser, of his Order of the Garter, his garterless stocking slips down, revealing a black and hairy simian leg. In 1914, meanwhile, the German cartoonist Arthur Johnson (his father was an American) showed the British Royal Family, German by descent, in a camp for enemy aliens.

These taunting cartoons bore little relation to the realities of modern warfare, and most of them would now be dismissed purely as rather ham-fisted propaganda. This shouldn't downplay their effectiveness, however.

A century earlier Napoleon Bonaparte admitted he feared the damage done by James Gillray's caricatures of him more than he feared any general, because Gillray always drew him as very short. (To bring this up to date, Le Monde's cartoonist Plantu told me that every time he drew Nicolas Sarkozy as short, Sarkozy complained personally to his editor; the next cartoon would make him even shorter, and Sarkozy would complain again, until in the end Plantu drew the French president as just a head and feet.)

Gag cartoons about the slapstick of everyday life in the trenches serve as another instance of humour being used to make the harshest imaginable reality simply bearable

Nonetheless, an unforeseen consequence of this barrage of caricature was that in the end people stopped believing it to be anything more than merely caricature: the truth that should be exposed by the exaggeration got lost. In the 1930s, many people assumed reports of the genuine atrocities of the Nazis were, like the bayoneted babies or harvested corpses blamed on the Kaiser, just propaganda.

Posterity shouldn't concern cartoonists. We're just journalists responding to events with a raw immediacy. This is what gives the medium a great deal of its heft.

Some cartoons, however, encapsulate a time or an event and so become part →

STRIPSEARCH
by MARTIN ROWSON
SO WHAT'S THIS THEN?
SHHH! IT'S A MONUMENT TO THE WAR FOUGHT FOR TRUTH & JUSTICE!
YOU WHAT?
2
HUSH! SHOW SOME RESPECT FOR THOSE WHO HEARD THE CALL & MADE THE ULTIMATE SACRIFICE TO SAVE US ALL FROM THE BABY-BAYONETTING HORDES OF ELDRITCH SUB-HUMAN MONKEY MEN BENT ON CEASELESS PILLAGE & RAPINE, SLAUGHTER & ETERNAL BONDAGE AND THE SNUFFING OUT OF THE LAST SPARK OF LIBERTY, HELD IN TRUST FOR ALL MANKIND IN THE STILL BEATING HEART OF THIS ISLAND REALM OF SWEET CHIVALRY!
UM... ARE YOU QUITE SURE ABOUT ALL THAT?
3
OF COURSE! THIS MONUMENT WAS ERECTED BY A GRATEFUL NATION TO HONOUR THAT GALLANT GENERATION WHO, IN OLDEN DAYS, GLADLY HURLED THEMSELVES THROUGH THE CRUEL CATS' CRADLES OF PLAITED BARBED WIRE INTO THE VERY MAW OF VALIANT MARTYRDOM, EMBRACING THE BULLETS' FATAL KISS FOR SIMPLE LOVE OF RIGHTEOUSNESS IN A JUST & HONOURABLE STRUGGLE FOR FREEDOM AND DEMOCRACY FOR EVERY SINGLE ONE OF US LEFT ALIVE!
REALLY? IN WHICH CASE...

4
...WHY IS THE GOVE MONUMENT TO THE EDUCATION WARS UNDER 24-HOUR ARMED GUARD TO KEEP THE PUBLIC OUT?
IDIOT! IT'S TO STOP THOSE PYONGYANG-TRAINED TROT TERROR PIGEONS ROOSTING ON HIS NOBLE BROW! ANYWAY, DID YOU KNOW THOSE EVIL MARXIST TEACHERS WERE PLANNING TO FORCE ALL PRIMARY SCHOOL PUPILS TO LEARN TO GOOSE STEP?!?
OH COME OFF IT! THAT'S JUST PROPAGANDA!
NO NO NO! NOT GANDERS - GEESE!
SIGH...
GAS
GAS

→ of the more general visual language. Gillray's The Plum Pudding in Danger is a perfect example, depicting the specific geopolitical struggle between William Pitt and Napoleon in 1805, while also capturing eternal truths about geopolitics itself. But I'm not aware of any political cartoons from World War I that do the same thing.

And yet the medium operates in many ways, and the most effective and popular cartoonist of World War I was undoubtedly Bruce Bainsfather, a serving artillery officer who drew gag cartoons about the slapstick of everyday life in the trenches in his series featuring "Old Bill". The serving soldiers loved these cartoons, and they are another instance of humour being used to make the harshest imaginable reality simply bearable.

The other truly great cartoon to emerge from the World War I was published after it was all over. In his extraordinarily prophetic drawing Peace and Future Cannon Fodder for the Daily Herald, Will Dyson showed the Allied victors of the war exiting the Versailles peace conference and the French prime minister Georges Clemenceau saying: "Curious! I seem to hear a child weeping." Behind a pillar a naked infant labelled "1940 class" is crying into its folded arms.

None of the protagonists in the next war doubted the power or importance of cartoons. Again, they were used by all sides to taunt and vilify their foes, perhaps most notoriously in Der Sturmer, the notorious anti-semitic paper edited by Julius Streicher, later hanged at Nuremburg.

Simplicissimus was, once more, taunting the British, this time drawing wartime prime minister, Winston Churchill, as a fat and murderous drunk; in the Soviet Union Stalin's favourite cartoonist, Boris Yefimov, returned the compliment to the Nazi leadership (Yefimov's older brother Mikhail first employed him on Pravda before being purged and executed in 1940; Boris survived him by 68 years, dying aged 108 in 2008). No cartoonist in either country would have dared caricature their own totalitarian politicians, but they were given full rein to exercise their skills on their nation's enemies. In Britain, with its largely legally tolerated history of visual satire going back to 1695, things were slightly different, though also sometimes the same.

The New Zealand-born cartoonist David Low discovered in 1930 from a friend that Hitler, three years away from taking power in Germany, was an admirer of his work. Low did what any other cartoonist would do in similar circumstances and acknowledged his famous fan by sending him a signed piece of original artwork, inscribed "From one artist to another".

It's unknown what happened to the cartoon – maybe it was with him right to the end, in the bunker – but it soon became apparent that Hitler had mistaken Low's attacks on democratic politicians for attacks on democracy itself. He was soon disabused. Low harried the Nazis all the way from the simple slapstick of The Difficulty of Shaking Hands with Gods of November 1933 to the bitterness of his iconic cartoon Rendezvous in September 1939, so much so that in 1936 British Foreign Secretary Lord Halifax, after a weekend's shooting at Hermann Goering's Bavarian hunting lodge, told Low's proprietor at the Evening Standard, Lord Beaverbrook, to get the cartoonist to ease up as his work was seriously damaging good Anglo-German relations. Low responded by producing a composite cartoon dictator called "Muzzler".

The Nazis had a point that Low entirely understood, and it was why he, along with many other cartoonists – Victor "Vicky" Weisz, Leslie Illingworth and even William Heath Robinson – were all on the Gestapo's death list. In a debate on British government propaganda in 1943, a Tory MP said Low's cartoon were worth all the official propaganda put together because Low portrayed the Nazis as "bloody fools". Low himself later expanded on the point, comparing his work, which undermined the Nazis through mockery, with the work of pre-war Danish cartoonists who unanimously drew them as terrifying monsters. Low's point was that it's much easier to imagine you can beat a fool than a monster, and taunting your enemies as being unvanguishably frightening is no taunt at all.

The enduring efficacy of cartoons' dark and magical voodoo powers were acknowledged in victory, when both Low and Yefimov were official court cartoonists at the Nuremburg war crimes tribunals (Low claimed Goering tried to outstare him from the dock): now the taunting was part of the humiliation served up with the revenge. Likewise, when Mussolini was executed by Italian partisans, the editor of the Evening Standard, Michael Foot, marked the dictator's demise by giving over all eight pages of the paper to Low's cartoons of Mussolini's life and career.

Of course Low, unlike Yefimov, was actively hostile on the Home Front as well, producing cartoons critical of both the military establishment and Churchill. When Low's famous creation Colonel Blimp, the portly cartoon manifestation of boneheaded reactionary thinking, took on fresh life in the Powell and Pressburger movie The Life and Death of Colonel Blimp, Churchill tried to have the film banned. When the Daily Mirror's cartoonist Philip Zec responded to stories about wartime profiteering by contrasting them with attacks on merchant shipping in his famous cartoon The Price of Petrol has Been Increased by One Penny – Official, both Churchill and Home Secretary Herbert Morrison seriously considered shutting down the newspaper. (When the Guardian cartoonist Les Gibbard pastiched Zec's cartoon during the Falklands war 40 years later, the Sun called for him to be tried for treason.)

And yet cartoons, for all their voodoo power, can still spiral off into all sorts of different ambiguities thanks to the way they inhabit different spheres of intent. Are they there to make us laugh, or to destroy them? Or both?

Ronald Searle drew his experiences while he was a prisoner of war of the Japanese, certainly on pain of death had the drawings been discovered, but taking the risk in order to stand witness to his captors' crimes. Just a few years later, many of his famous St Trinian's cartoons don't just deal with the same topics – cruelty and beheadings – but share identical composition with his prisoner of war drawings.

And when Carl Giles, creator of the famous cartoon family that mapped and reflected post-war British suburban life

Low and Yefimov were official court cartoonists at the Nuremburg war crimes tribunals

weekly in the Sunday Express, was present as an official war correspondent at the liberation of the Bergen-Belsen concentration camp, the camp's commandant, Josef Kramer, revealed he was a huge fan of Giles' work and gave him his pistol, a ceremonial dagger and his Nazi armband in exchange for the promise that Giles would send him a signed original. As Giles explained later, he failed to keep his part of the bargain because by the time he got demobbed Kramer had been hanged for crimes against humanity.

Those twinned qualities of taunting and laughter go some way to explaining the experience of cartoonists in the so-called war on terror, if not the power of their work. In the aftermath of 9/11, in the Babel of journalistic responses to what was without question the most visual event in human history, then visually re-repeated by the media that had initially reported it, the cartoonists were the ones who got it in the neck. →

→ While columnists wrote millions of words of comment and speculation, and images captured by machines were broadcast and published almost ceaselessly, the images produced via a human consciousness were, it seems, too much to stomach for many. Cartoonists had their work spiked, or were told to cover another story (there were no other stories). In the US some cartoonists had their copy moved to other parts of the paper, or were laid off. One or two even got a knock on the door in the middle of the night from the Feds under the provisions of the Patriot Act.

Despite a concerted effort by some American strip cartoonists to close ranks on Thanksgiving Day 2001 and show some patriotic backbone, the example of Beetle Bailey flying on the back of an American Eagle didn't really act as a general unifier. Unlike in previous wars, there was no unanimity of purpose among cartoonists. An editorial in The Daily Telegraph accused me, along with Dave Brown of The Independent and The Guardian's Steve Bell, of being "useful idiots" aiding the terrorist cause due to our failure to fall in line.

The war on terror and its Iraqi sideshow were anything but consensus wars, and many cartoonists articulated very loudly their misgivings. These included Peter Brookes of the Murdoch-owned Times drawing cartoons in direct opposition to his paper's editorial line. This has always been one of visual satire's greatest strengths: sometimes a cartoon can undermine itself.

Moreover, because a majority of cartoons were back in their comfort zone of oppositionism, the taunting had less of the whiff of propaganda about it. Nor was there ever any suggestion in Britain of government censorship of any of this.

That said, the volume of censuring increased exponentially, thanks entirely to the separate but simultaneous growth in digital communication and social media. Whereas, previously, cartoons might elicit an outraged letter to an editor – let alone a death threat from the Gestapo – the internet allowed a global audience to see material to which thousands of people responded, thanks to email, with concerted deluges of hate email and regular death threats. I long since learned to dismiss an email death threat as meaningless – a real one requires the commitment of finding my address, a stamp and possibly a body part of one of my loved ones – but it's the thought that counts.

More to the point was the second front in the culture-struggle at the heart of the war on terror, in which both sides fought to take greater offence. Amid the bombs, bullets and piles of corpses across Iraq, Afghanistan, Bali, Madrid, London and all the other places, the greatest harm you could suffer, it seemed was that you might be "offended". People sent me hate emails and threatened to kill me and my children because they were "offended" by my depiction of George Bush, or by a cartoon criticising Israel, or a stupid humourous drawing of anything that might mildly upset them or their beliefs.

It was into this atmosphere that the row over the cartoons of Mohammed published by the Danish newspaper Jyllands Posten erupted, resulting in the deaths of at least 100 people (none of them cartoonists, but most of them Muslims, and many shot dead by Muslim soldiers or policemen). But that, of course, is another story. And – who knows? – may yet prove to be another war. X

Martin Rowson's cartoons appear regularly in The Guardian and Index on Censorship. His books include The Dog Allusion, Giving Offence and Fuck: the Human Odyssey

Weapons of disinformation

43(1): 41/44 | DOI: 10.1177/0306422014521742

Daniel Carter looks back on Pinochet's Chile and the role of a media empire in the military dictator's propaganda machine. Its high circulation newspapers justified and provoked a military coup in a country previously famed for strong democratic traditions, and then actively collaborated with the regime

THE DAY WILL not be easily forgotten in Chile. September 11 1973 saw the violent overthrow of democratically elected Chilean President Salvador Allende and the installation of one of the longest of Latin America's 20th century military dictatorships.

In Chile during the 1960s, a consensus in favour of radical modernisation policies had emerged across much of the political spectrum. Policies including the redistribution of land to peasants or the nationalisation of wealth-generating resources such as copper represented an existential threat to the closely knit families who had historically controlled most of that wealth, along with the political power deriving from it. A key name in the pantheon of Chilean oligarchs is the Edwards family, owners since 1849 of their country's largest circulation daily newspaper, El Mercurio, and a number of local and national subsidiaries.

One feature that makes the Chilean case stand out among the military regimes that held much of Latin America in their grip during the last third of the 20th century is the role of the media – and in particular El Mercurio and its subsidiaries – in consciously promoting a perceived state of war, both before and after the coup which brought General Augusto Pinochet to power. The planting of exaggerated or invented reports on foreign infiltration, unsubstantiated warnings about scarcity of basic goods (which became a self-fulfilling prophecy as a result of panic buying) or false revelations of sinister leftist plots was, by most historical accounts, a major factor in both justifying and provoking a military coup in a country previously famed for its strong democratic traditions. A logical consequence of the mission to bring down a president whose political opinions differed too much from their own was the paper's subsequent role as mouthpiece for the Pinochet regime, along with the consistent covering up of crimes committed by the dictatorship until the transition to democracy in 1990.

A film, made by students of the School of Journalism at the University of Chile in 2008 (El Diario de Agustín by Ignacio Agüero, 2008, referring to Agustín Edwards, founder and owner of El Mercurio), tells the story of how a paper that claimed to campaign for freedom and to prevent what it saw as the seeds of totalitarianism ended up destroying democracy and actively collaborating in crimes against human rights. It features interviews with journalists, commentators, the →

→ paper's directors and victims of human rights abuses.

Near the beginning of the film, prize-winning sociologist Manuel Antonio Garretón argues that El Mercurio transformed itself from a traditional conservative daily newspaper dedicated to forming public opinion into an element dedicated to political destabilisation. Already in 1967, years before the election of Allende, mass mobilisation by students and peasants was being supported by the Christian Democrat administration of Eduardo Frei, giving way to sweeping reforms that opened the gates to universal education and mass land ownership. According to Garretón, El Mercurio understood what was at stake, causing it to take up an extreme position that made it "not only into anti-Allende newspaper, but also an anti-democratic newspaper, basically a promoter of military takeover." Stories began to run, falsely and deliberately implicating international communism in domestic student protest movements. Declassified documents released by the CIA in 1999 and analysed by Peter Kornbluh in The Pinochet File: A Declassified Dossier on Atrocity and Accountability, clearly demonstrate that the organisation had poured money into El Mercurio throughout the 1960s to prevent a left-wing victory, paying journalists to write opinion columns and articles for placement.

A paper that claimed to campaign for freedom and to prevent what it saw as the seeds of totalitarianism ended up destroying democracy and actively collaborating in crimes against human rights

In September 1970, the same month that Salvador Allende achieved the narrow electoral victory that would enable him to become the world's first democratically elected Marxist president, Agustín Edwards met leading members of the CIA and the White House to discuss how best to get rid of Allende. According to Kornbluh, "throughout Allende's aborted tenure, the paper continued an unyielding campaign, running countless virulent, inflammatory articles and editorials exhorting opposition against — and at times even calling for the overthrow of — the Popular Unity government."

Although the campaign had failed to prevent Allende winning power, it succeeded in rallying a supposedly impartial military to take over power to "restore order". However, the most blatant use of lies and propaganda occurred in the aftermath of military intervention. The coup, symbolised by the startling attack on the presidential palace, La Moneda, whose burning façade after the air strike is, for some, among the last century's most iconic images, rapidly became synonymous with reports of mass arrests and disappearances. In order to justify this audacious act in the eyes of the world, as well as to ensure compliance amongst its own population, an entirely fabricated leftist plot, known as Plan Z, was announced by El Mercurio and one of its subsidiaries, Las Ultimas Noticias, less than a week after the coup. The alleged plan involved a military operation by Allende supporters to murder members of the armed forces and their families, import illegal arms and reduce Chile to chaos. A series of headlines followed, in order to emphasise the magnitude of the alleged operation: "600 families to be assassinated in Concepcion"; "Marxists planned the destruction of Limache" (a town near Valpaiso); "Another guerrilla training school discovered." The existence of Plan Z has now been shown conclusively to be a fabrication. My own investigations of the coup in the southern provinces of Chile have shown that "guerrilla training schools" were little more than peasant co-operatives, which, at most, possessed a few rudimentary shotguns as a means of self-defence against hostile ex-landowners.

During the long dictatorship that followed, all opposition newspapers were banned, giving the Mercurio group an unrivalled market position, which it had not enjoyed before. But instead of using this privilege to soften the impact of military rule over an often terrified population, by reporting on crimes such as torture, murder or kidnap carried out by Pinochet sympathisers, El Mercurio chose to cover up those crimes by actively collaborating in a disinformation campaign. El Diario de Agustín depicts several examples of this.

Perhaps the most dramatic is the "Case of the 119", a reference to an extraordinary cover-up operation to hide the practice of forced disappearance of political activists carried out by the regime's semi-clandestine police unit, the National Intelligence Directorate (DINA). On 12 June 1975, La Segunda, a paper in the Mercurio group, published a front-page headline claiming that 2,000 Marxists were training in Argentina to organise guerrilla activities against Chile, including those who were believed to be "missing". Various papers subsequently ran stories about arrests of dangerous terrorists and of guerrilla movements in Argentina as a prelude to the grand finale: that 60 of them had died in fratricidal in-fighting, and, separately, that 59 had been "exterminated like rats" by the Argentine secret services. Research by human rights groups and subsequently by the Chilean justice system, demonstrated that the information had originated in Santiago, and that bogus editions of non-existent magazines had been set up in Brazil and Argentina to report the stories. The Argentine secret services even collaborated by supplying dead bodies, which it was happy to identify as belonging to Chilean subversives. The lengths to which the secret services went to cover up its crimes by creating a false narrative of war, along with fake sources – with the active participation of the Mercurio newspaper group – demonstrates how concerned they were to keep secret the policy of forced disappearance.

ABOVE: Soldiers in Valparaiso, 15 days after Augusto Pinochet's coup, September 1973. Following the coup, the military junta burned material they deemed as being against the regime

Credit: Sipa Press/Rex Features

A dramatic story appearing a year later concerned the supposed case of a young woman who had been murdered on a beach in central Chile's fifth region in a case of *crime passionnel*. According to El Mercurio, the body, discovered in September 1976, belonged to a 23-year-old woman who had been raped, beaten and dragged onto the beach at Los Molles, well known as a refuge for young lovers. The story hid a more sinister reality, however. The body in fact →

→ belonged to Marta Ugarte, a 42-year-old member of the Communist Party who, like hundreds of her fellow activists, had been taken from the infamous Villa Grimaldi torture centre and dumped at sea from army helicopters, in an operation known as the "death flights". Human rights organisations estimate that some 400 prisoners of the DINA met this fate. Hers was the only body which ever returned to land. Testimonies by air force personnel responsible for the crime indicate that she became detached from the rail that was meant to ensure her body sank. Interviewed for El Diario de Agustín, Juan Guzman, the judge who presided over the case, affirmed that El Mercurio was a key instrument in the dictatorship's crimes. The view was confirmed by the reporter assigned to cover the story, who claimed that press releases emanated directly from personnel within the secret services However when Arturo Fontaine, sub director of El Mercurio 1965-1978, was interviewed for the film and was asked if staff ever questioned their sources he said: "We were not handed information. We had our own sources. I am relatively proud of that. Do not think I am not."

The author of this article approached El Mercuio for a comment, but the media group did not respond.

There is evidence that El Mercurio remained as complicit at the end of the dictatorship as it had been at the beginning. A visit to Chile by Pope John Paul II in 1987 nearly turned into a public relations disaster for the regime, when teargas hurled at demonstrators outside the stadium where he was speaking began to affect those inside, including the Pope himself. El Mercurio ran an article the following day, which claimed that trouble had been stirred up deliberately by members of the communist party. Photos of the two "instigators" appeared on the front page.—The paper claimed to have identified them from a "thorough revision of photographs and videos shot during the disturbances." As a result of these allegations, the two men were taken from their homes, arrested and tortured. Even government sources were unsure of the reliability of information emitted by the National Information Centre (CNI), a supposedly more respectable secret police unit that had replaced the infamous DINA in 1978. In spite of these official doubts, the paper went ahead with publication of the photos, resulting in the arrest and torture of two young men who had not even been present at the demonstration.

By contrast to the absolute freedom enjoyed by the regime's press officers and their willing accomplices in El Mercurio, critical journalism was silenced through closure, censorship and murder. According to Puro Chile, a webpage that takes its name from a newspaper whose offices were destroyed by the military on the day of the coup, the dictatorship assassinated or "disappeared" a total of 23 journalists, nine journalism students, 20 photographers, and a number of others associated with the trade, totalling over 100. In 2006, a monument to these victims was erected in the headquarters of the Chilean Guild of Journalists in the capital, Santiago. Their voices had not only been proscribed, but silenced forever. Perhaps, in the case of Chile between 1967 and 1990, the truth was not so much a casualty of war as a victim of cold-blooded assassination by the country's oligarchs. ☒

Daniel Carter teaches at Cambridge University and completed a PhD at the Centre of Latin American Studies focusing on social conflict in the province of Cautín from 1967-1973. He has contributed to the journal Studies in Ethnicity and Nationalism (Wiley) and is currently researching the role of social movements in Spain's transition to democracy

Call to arms

43(1): 45/49 | DOI: 10.1177/0306422014523380

Leanne Green looks at the story behind the iconic poster campaigns of World War I and mass media's role

NEW TECHNOLGIES AND methods of distribution had changed the face of the nineteenth century printing industry and created new, wider readerships. As a result, World War I was the first conflict in which the mass media played a significant role.

In 1914 Britain witnessed for the first time the new phenomenon of national governments adopting the techniques of advertising to promote war aims, both domestically and globally. Reported in daily newspapers weekly journals, publicised through posters, and pamphlets and commercial advertising

It is arguably little wonder that World, War I became known as the first "total war" - executed at first hand by soldiers conscripted en masse and experienced by entire populations on the home front. While our own historical vantage point allows us to consider the war with knowledge of the consequences and effects it had on society, it must also be situated on a continuum with an earlier phase. World War I was born out of a long nineteenth century that witnessed increasing industrialization and urbanization and the rise of mass media. Thus, when war descended on Europe, printing, the archetype of mass production, became as relevant as the manufacturing of munitions. Reaching large numbers of people, propaganda posters conveyed the war aims of the British government, and aimed at persuading civilian populations that their collective effort would be essential to securing victory.

But perhaps surprisingly given the relative sophistication of the British advertising industry by 1914 and the scale of the propaganda campaign by 1918, the adoption of a full-scale poster campaign was at the time a step taken tentatively by the British government. The poster campaigns of political parties for the 1910 general election had established a premise for large scale canvassing, but posters were an object of criticism. Abundantly displayed in public spaces, the erection of signs and hoardings provoked an organised public reaction in the form of the National Society for Controlling the Abuses of Public Advertising, its membership list containing a number of notable names including William Morris and Rudyard Kipling. (Although opinions differed; The Times argued in 1892 that: "They cause a great deal of pleasure to a great many persons who live very dull lives, and in a very large number of instances their →

When war descended on Europe printing became as relevant as the manufacturing of munitions

ABOVE: The iconic World War I propaganda poster designed by Alfred Leete

Credit: London Opinion/Victoria House Publishing/IWM London

→ surroundings are already so hideous that they cannot be made worse"). But it was the poster's tendency to importune passers-by with commercial appeals that attracted criticism; it was thought to be in poor taste. Once war broke out, the poster gained a new, legitimised role as a vehicle for official propaganda, freeing it from the usual air of hostility and distaste.

One of the first aims of Britain's propaganda machinery was to convince a divided nation of a justification for war. In the years leading up to 1914 Suffragette militancy, industrial action and the issue of home rule in Ireland had taken form in social unrest. With the German invasion of Belgium on 4 August 1914, Britain established a noble cause, with newspaper headlines lamenting "Poor Little Belgium"; not only had Germany violated an international treaty in their invasion of neutral land, according to press reports they were showing no remorse as they committed alleged acts of atrocity upon the innocent nation. Fully aware of the usefulness of the Belgian cause in garnering support for British involvement, the earliest declarations of war aims were almost always made in speeches about Belgium. On the day that Britain declared war, Sir Edward Grey implored: "If, in a crisis like this, we ran away from our obligations of honour and interest with regard to the Belgian treaty, I doubt, whatever material force we might have at the end, whether it would be of very much value in face of the respect we would have lost." Early visual propaganda presented images of Belgium as an innocent child or a woman ravaged by "the Hun", and recruitment posters implored men to "Remember Belgium" and asked, "Have you any womenfolk worth defending?" The violation of Belgium was one of the most powerful inducements for men to enlist, with government propaganda promoting a feeling that this was a justified war against a monstrous enemy.

And it was not only government-produced material that featured this kind of imagery. Charity materials made for the Red Cross and the Belgian Canal Boat Fund, amongst other organisations, drew on similar gendered rhetoric to garner support, portraying images of displaced women and children. By placing an emphasis on gendered representations of domestic safety, the meaning of war could be explained in humanitarian terms. It was not uncommon to see prominent members of government on the boards of wartime charities, implementing a type of government policy by proxy. The distinctions between a recruiting poster that aimed to sell the army and a charitable advertisement soliciting donations became fewer as the aims of different concerns became symbiotic. With the press also justifying the war in terms of the sanctity of the law and the safety of civilians, Britain's involvement became difficult to dispute.

The parties in the 1910 general election used poster campaigns for large scale canvassing

Just as the issue of gaining support for the war necessitated adopting the plight of Belgium as a selling point, convincing the British public of the idea of conscription called for another of the government's most extensive campaigns. The German and French armies were made up of conscripted soldiers, but by contrast, the British Army was smaller, and consisted of professional soldiers and volunteers. The notion of conscription was deeply opposed in British society, it being somewhat paradoxical for the British to claim to be fighting for freedom in the name of liberal democracy, with an army made up of men who had been forced to fight. Instead, men had to be sold a picture of life in the British army that would encourage them to join. Had the government introduced conscription before doing so, it is likely that →

→ the war wouldn't have received the support it did from the British public. The Parliamentary Recruitment Committee (PRC) was established to sell the idea of conscription to the British public, and between October 1914 and July 1916 they produced some of the most memorable images of World War I.

The earliest recruitment posters were adorned with only the Royal monogram and the words "England expects every man to do his duty", but as the campaign progressed techniques of persuasion became increasingly sophisticated. Members of the advertising community worked with the government to help the state appropriate advertising techniques to sell the war effectively. The war cabinet relied on advertising experts such as Hadley Le Bas, Thomas Russell and Charles Higham to ensure campaigns achieved the desired result. Relationships between British and American advertisers allowed ideas to filter across the Atlantic, and British advertising mirrored the persuasive techniques used in the United States. Poster such as "Daddy, what did YOU do in the war?" emotionally manipulated the viewer, playing on personal relationships and basic human anxieties. These tactics were sharpened as war went on, and were crucial in the attempt to attract men to the war machine.

The distinctive design of Lord Kitchener's penetrating glare and pointing finger in the famous World War I recruitment poster is one of the most enduring wartime propaganda images. The poster instructs potential recruits that "Kitchener needs YOU!", referencing then Secretary of State for War Lord Kitchener, a national hero whose exploits in the Sudan were lauded in the press and celebrated in the popular adventure fiction of GA Henty. However, although we now think of this as one of the most common propaganda posters used for recruitment, archivist Nicholas Hiley has convincingly argued that his image may not have been as prevalent during the war as claims have led us to believe. The image we know today was actually originally designed by graphic artist Alfred Leete, for publication on the cover of London Opinion magazine. Little reference is made to Leete's design in the files of the PRC, or in the war office or the public accounts of David Allen and Sons' wartime work, indicating that it was never actually used as a propaganda poster during the war. Instead references to Kitchener's face appearing "on every hoarding" may well refer to another poster produced in July 1915 showing the war minister's stern glare beside the searching question "Does the call of duty find no response in you until reinforced?" The later poster was issued in two different sizes, and had a large print run of 145,000, making it the most numerous of all the PRC posters. It was hung in the PRC's Downing Street office and mentioned in the official summary of the committee's work, neither of these honours being conferred to the London Opinion poster.

Money making propaganda

By July 1916, the introduction of conscription rendered the PRC obsolete and with little hope of an end to the war in sight, the government's propaganda campaign shifted towards maintaining morale. Propaganda efforts focused on the "Call to arms" to encourage industrial activity, the conservation of food, and economic appeals. Throughout the war, the aim was never to change opinion, but to maintain interest. Thus, once the initial excitement had passed, more emotionally manipulative techniques were necessary. This change in tone was often reflected in an increased use of guilt as a method of persuasion. In appealing for male and female munitions workers, the posters maintained a positive outlook, exclaiming "We're both needed to serve the guns!". Towards 1916, when the government's need to raise money increased, the worker's honour was called into question. One poster implored, "You earn more than he does" to encourage workers to purchase war savings. The close ties between commerce and government became increasingly clear through seeing commercial interests directly promoting government agendas. Waterman's Fountain Pens encouraged their customers to use "the finest writing instrument for signing your application for National War Bonds" and Quaker Oats exclaimed that, "A £5 Bond hits the Kaiser harder than 5000 words". The tone of economic appeals changed, becoming more forthright and graphic. Frank Brangwyn's poster reading "Put strength in the final blow", which portrays a British soldier pinning a German soldier to the ground with his bayonet, is unusual in its depiction of the violence of war. The image links our financial investment with the soldier striking the blow, our money giving him the strength to commit his violent act.

The ultimate aim of Britain's poster propaganda campaign was to maintain support and interest in a long and drawn out war, and it did so by adopting the techniques of advertising to seduce its audience on a social and cultural level. Propaganda was an instrumental link between the state and the masses, and it allowed Britain's war aims to penetrate all facets of daily life. Facilitated by the relationships between government, the press, and the advertising industry, the war was inescapable. It featured in breakfast cereal advertising and it adorned the walls and hoardings along the commute to work. In many ways the twentieth century began in 1914 - not for the political, social and technological changes the war brought about, but for the beginnings of the media and consumer driven society we live in today. ☒

Leanne Green is a collaborative doctoral researcher and associate lecturer at Imperial War Museum London and MIRIAD, Manchester Metropolitan University

'La France libre, 1918' © National WWI Museum at Liberty Memorial Archives, Kansas City, Missouri, USA

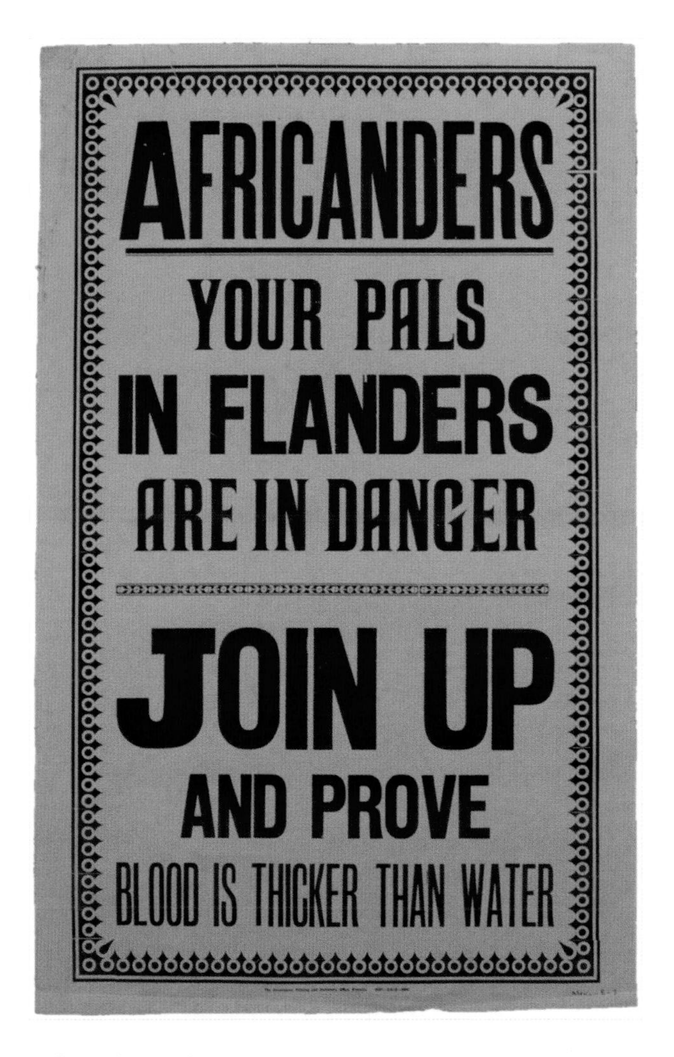

'Africanders, n.d.'

© National WWI Museum at Liberty Memorial Archives, Kansas City, Missouri, USA

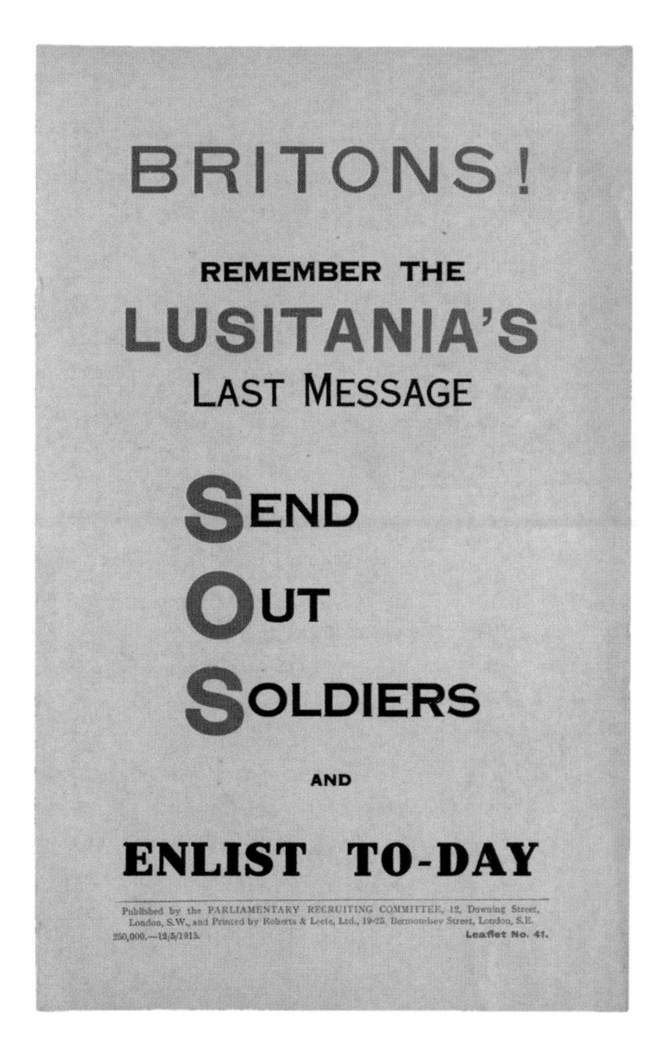

'Britons! Remember the Lusitania's Last Message! 12 May 1915'

© The William Ready Division of Archives and Research Collections at McMaster University, Canada

All images from **'The First World War: Propaganda and Recruitment'** ©Adam Matthew Digital Ltd 2013, www.amdigital.co.uk

Bonds of war

43(1): 52/55 | DOI: 10.1177/0306422014522915

A campaign of pro-German propaganda massively backfired against the German-American community in World War I, **Sally Gimson** follows the story through the pages of The Fatherland magazine

A BACKLASH AGAINST THE German-American community in WWI ended with German words being banned, and Berlin, Michigan, being renamed. The word hamburger was even dropped and replaced by "liberty steak".

To help trace the little known tale of efforts to persuade the United States to support Germany during the war, Index on Censorship was given special access to the digital collection, Propaganda and Recruitment, which includes all the copies printed of The Fatherland magazine, a publication started in New York in August 1914 by George Sylvester Viereck, an American citizen who became the German government's most ardent apologist in the US. By the time the US entered the war in April 1917, Washington's own much more powerful and sophisticated propaganda machine had turned its fire against them.

As US President Woodrow Wilson put it in his Flag Day speech in June that year in Washington: "The military masters of Germany...filled our unsuspecting communities with vicious spies and conspirators and sought to corrupt the opinion of our people." German agents, he declared, had "diligently spread sedition among us and sought to draw our own citizens from their allegiance".

Seven million copies of this speech were distributed by the government's Committee on Public Information. It marked the escalation of a vicious campaign against German-Americans. In that same month Congress passed the Espionage Act, followed by the Sedition Act in 1918 (repealed in December 1921), which prohibited "disloyal, profane, scurrilous or abusive language about the form of government of the United States". America had gone to war in Europe after staying neutral for three years, and now needed to bind Americans together in the war effort.

At the turn of the twentieth century, German-Americans were the largest non-English-speaking ethnic group in the US. According to the 1910 census they numbered eight million out of a total population of 92 million, and comprised a quarter of the white population. They were the most numerous ethnic group in cities such as Baltimore, Chicago, Cincinnati, Detroit, Los Angeles and Milwaukee.

Many were well-assimilated, but there was also a strong culture of clubs and churches. By the 1890s there were nearly 800 German-language newspapers and journals in America. Although this had fallen to 522 by 1917, there were still almost as many German-language publications as in all other foreign languages combined.

ABOVE: A group gathers to show the various Washington D.C. newspaper headlines on November 11 1918, the day World War I ended

Credit: Nara Archives/Rex

The earliest German settlers arrived in 1708. They were Palatines fleeing religious persecution, and settled as farmers in Pennsylvania, New York, Maryland, Virginia and the Carolinas. A second wave of German immigration began after 1830, growing pace after the 1848 revolutions in Europe, and a third wave, 1.7 million, came between 1881 and 1892 when the German economy was depressed.

Frederick Luebke, whose book Bonds of Loyalty is the only useful survey of German-Americans during World War I, argues that most people's political loyalties always lay with the United States. But from the outbreak of war in Europe in 1914, even though the USA had declared neutrality, it would never be the same for German-Americans.

Anglo-Saxon Americans believed the Kaiser was intent on world domination and would use all means at his disposal to achieve his aims. Many German-Americans were unable or unwilling to understand that this was the general view. Most, at least at the beginning, supported Wilson because they did not want to go to war. →

→ But some saw neutrality as an admission of weakness, and an opportunity to bind the German-American community together by appealing to an anti-British German nationalism.

It was a view the pro-German magazine The Fatherland propagated. George Viereck used the magazine, which boasted the strapline Devoted to Fair Play For Germany and Austria, to try to educate Americans in the virtues of the German position and show the basic bad faith of the Allies. By October 1914 its circulation was 100,000.

A cartoon in The Fatherland on 30 September 1914 shows the Iron Cross and the Union Jack with the rubric: "Two Crosses of totally different standards: the German Imperial Cross and the well-known Double Cross of Great Britain."

In August 1915 a German agent left a briefcase detailing Germany's propaganda effort in a carriage in a railway carriage on Sixth Avenue in New York

Viereck used the pages of his paper to raise money for German war bonds. In New York, the German Historical Society inaugurated a war relief fund by selling rings bearing the Iron Cross, which were advertised in The Fatherland. Newspapers of the time said thousands of New Yorkers exchanged jewelry and cash for the rings, which bore the inscription: "To show my loyalty to the old Fatherland, I brought it gold in time of trouble for this piece of iron."

German propaganda was, however, incompetent. The gravest error happened over the sinking of the passenger steamer Lusitania in May 1915. On the day the Lusitania sailed for Liverpool, the German ambassador in America authorised the embassy in Washington to place an advertisement in the New York Times warning that any ship flying the flag of Great Britain and in waters round the British isles was liable to be destroyed.

This notice appeared next to a Cunard advertisement for the Lusitania, days before it was sunk by a German submarine off the southern coast of Ireland with the loss of 1,200 lives – including 124 American citizens.

An earlier political bungle was a lobbying effort led by German-Americans to impose an embargo on all arms sales including those to Britain. American companies were making a lot of money in arms sales and armament exports, and a conference in support of the proposed embargo in January 1915 turned into a fiasco. The men who ran the conference, including Viereck, were condemned by the New York Times as "agents of German propaganda", as indeed they were.

The embargo campaign allowed President Wilson to attack German-Americans as being "hyphenates", people who had divided loyalties.

In August 1915, a German agent left a briefcase full of papers detailing Germany's propaganda effort in a carriage of the Sixth Avenue elevated railway in New York. It was picked up by the secret service agent tailing him. When Secretary of the Treasury William McAdoo saw the documents, he realised they were gold dust and made sure the most damaging elements were published in the New York World.

The episode was catastrophic for the German propaganda effort because it dramatised spying accusations that were already rife. Every half-baked plan the Germans were considering was revealed, including buying up munitions factories and organising strikes to prevent arms shipments to the allies.

By April 1917, when America entered the war, German-Americans were irrevocably tainted. However much they protested their loyalty, with German newspapers across the country placing American flags and patriotic poetry on their front pages, they were suspected of being traitors. The American government's propaganda campaign, led by the journalist George Creel's Committee on Public Information, was large, brutal and repressive. Creel himself, who after the war wrote a book called How We Advertised America, freely admitted that "an open mind is not part of my inheritance. I took in prejudices with mother's milk and was weaned on partisanship".

German-Americans found themselves obliged to give up any German connections, even if they were just cultural, and swear public loyalty to the US.Any criticism or discussion of the rights and wrongs of the American government's position on war was criminalised as sedition.

Laws were enacted to restrict German instruction in American schools. German church schools were shut down. The German language press disappeared. German university professors were dismissed for making disloyal statements. On 5 April 1918, in Collinsville, Illinois, Robert Prager, an immigrant who had arrived from Dresden in 1905, was lynched. His murderers were tried and found not guilty. Seldom in the history of Western propaganda can a campaign have proved so counter-productive and destructive as the attempt by the German Reich and German-Americans to rally anti-British opinion.

Sally Gimson is a former freelance Berlin correspondent for the Sunday Times and a former news producer at Deutsche Welle TV

Carnage on the Clyde

43(1): 56/60 | DOI: 10.1177/0306422014522579

When the Luftwaffe flattened the small Scottish shipbuilding town of Clydebank in one of the most destructive bombing raids of World War II, official censors went to quite extraordinary lengths to suppress reporting of the scale of the disaster. **John MacLeod** tells the story

ON A FINE moonlit evening on Thursday 13 March 1941, just after 9pm, the first of 236 German bombers converged on Clydeside. By 9.10pm, over the western suburbs of Glasgow, over Bowling and Dalnottar and – especially – over the crowded, densely housed and productive little town of Clydebank, the bombs had begun to fall. And the next night, it happened all over again.

This was bombing of such ferocity that the explosions could be heard clearly at Bridge of Allan in Stirlingshire. The fires were of such frenzy that their glow could be clearly seen from rural Aberdeenshire and Northern Ireland.

Clydebank was all but destroyed. According to the official statistics, 528 people - from one geographically small community - were killed, 617 seriously injured. Hundreds, perhaps thousands, more were superficially hurt and cut, or traumatised by blasts. Of some 12,000 dwellings – including tenement blocks as well as villas and semi-detached homes – only seven were left entirely undamaged. Four thousand homes were completely destroyed, and 4,500 more were so severely damaged as to be uninhabitable for months.

The morning of the 14 March saw thousands of dazed survivors shambling along Dumbarton Road into Glasgow and, by the night of Saturday 15 March – as official records would eventually reveal – it was reckoned that more than 40,000 people had left the town amid utter chaos.

In the days immediately following the German assault, soldiers and servicemen came home on leave to Clydebank wholly innocent of what had happened. John Bowman, in March 2011, bleakly recalled - for a BBC Scotland audience - returning from his distant base in Sussex to find not only his house obliterated, but most of the street; and that his mother, two brothers and a younger sister had been killed.

There is still a place called Clydebank, and many who survived March 1941 still live there. But thousands who fled never returned. The community that had retired for the evening of Thursday 13 March 1941 was smashed beyond recovery in a single night in what, in proportion of lives lost and homes destroyed, was the worst bombing raid anywhere in Britain in the entire war. Clydebank, the historian Angus Calder bleakly noted in 1969, "had the honour of suffering the most nearly universal damage of any British town".

But, outside Scotland, few have ever heard of the Clydebank Blitz. The Blitz, to most today, conjures up images of heroic London and battered Coventry – the first because it

ABOVE: A destroyed tram is surrounded by the rubble from fallen houses. Dumbarton Road, Clydebank, was almost unrecognisable following the raid

Credit: West Dunbartonshire Libraries and Cultural Services

was, of course, the capital; and the second because the authorities deliberately exploited its ordeal for newsreel propaganda.

Of course very many towns and cities were bombed. Those particularly hard-hit included Liverpool, Hull, Southampton and Belfast. Besides, Clydebank is readily confused with the vague term "Clydeside", used to describe the greater Glasgow area. But – beyond that – there was calculated wartime censorship by what was laughably known as the Ministry of Information.

Officials refused to allow any mention of the town's name in subsequent newspaper reports – which only speak of the bombing of "a town in western Scotland". No film-crews were allowed into the ruins. Neither royalty nor Prime Minister Winston Churchill sped north to visit and console. And, when one survivor, Thomas Kearns, wrote a detailed letter to family in Belfast, it was intercepted (and held) by censors. His words would not see publication till 1971.

A stark photograph, days later, of a Clydebank mass burial, was cropped before publication – on ministry orders – so that the public would not grasp just how terrible the disaster had been; 67 people, or bits of →

→ them, lay in it. And the government did its best, at first not to issue casualty figures at all, and then to give most misleading ones.

On 18 March 1941 the Ministry of Home Security – headed by Home Secretary Herbert Morrison – issued a foolish communiqué declaring that "about 500 persons had been killed on the raids in Clydeside". In fact, 647 had died in Glasgow alone – quite apart from the Clydebank death-toll – and, on hearing of this fatuous announcement, a Home Guardsman in Clydebank is said bitterly to have exclaimed: "Which street?"

Bureaucrats seem to have been determined deliberately to conflate Clydebank and Glasgow fatalities, to the point where the home secretary was accused in the House of Commons of making "misleading statements". Inevitably, feelings around Clydebank ran high.

Of some 12,000 dwellings, including tenement blocks as well as villas and semi-detached homes, only seven were left undamaged

A high official warned Tom Johnston, secretary of state for Scotland, that locals heard such official statistics with "frank incredulity" and, a year on, there was great consternation in high places when a Sunday Post anniversary piece, on 15 March 1942, lamented the "1,200 Clydebank people" who had died "as the result of the savage two-night blitz on the town".

This article had somehow evaded censors. Clydebank Burgh Council now held a furious debate, in which all sides demanded hard, accurate numbers from the government.

But these it refused to yield for the rest of the war. Thus, to this day, many regard the official death toll, as at last made known, with profound scepticism – especially when, decades after the attack, human remains were still being found in Clydebank rubble.

Such games of officialdom were not unique to the Clydebank catastrophe. As the historian Peter Lewis dryly notes, after the dreadful bombing of Manchester on 22 and 23 December 1940 The Manchester Guardian "was not allowed to name the city in its reports of the raids on 'an inland town in north-west England' or state that 'a newspaper office' hit by incendiaries was its own. Only when the Germans boasted of hitting Manchester was Manchester entitled to be told how heavy the raids and the damage were."

Hull, the worst-bombed city in England, likewise grew inured to being described as "an east-coast town", even as sailors came home on leave and lamented through incessant raids that they felt safer at sea. Yet the suppression of detail on Clydebank's ordeal was determined and exceptional.

There were four evident reasons for this. The first was military. The Clyde generally was a vital workshop for ships, munitions and ordnance. Clydebank was of particular importance, notably for the great yard of John Brown's. The authorities genuinely believed the Germans should never be told what they had actually hit, far less missed, lest they return and make good their failures.

The second was mortification. Though the imminent attack had been known for hours by the authorities, no warning of any kind had been given the people until German aircraft were practically within earshot. RAF tactics for the defence of greater Glasgow on those nights – too complex to discuss here – had been a humiliating failure. The scant anti-aircraft guns by Clydebank had run out of ammunition. Scottish Office officials had treated the town so contemptuously that Clydebank could not bury her dead even in cardboard coffins; most who were finally deposited in that huge grave were in bedsheets tied with string.

A third undoubted concern was the spectre of Scottish nationalism. Tom Johnston had talked it up at every opportunity in the pursuit of London largesse, especially after a succession of witless mistakes. The BBC had ended all Scottish regional broadcasting when war began. The new BBC Home Service then persisted, for months, in the incessant playing of There'll Always Be An England and authority at every level persisted stubbornly on using "English" as a synonym for British. In a spectacular gaffe – when a newsreel described the unambiguously Scottish RAF hero Donald Farquhar as an "English airman", there was booing throughout Scottish cinemas.

The final factor was a baseless fear of Marxist sedition. Clydeside was an early – and, by 1941, the most organised – fortress of British socialism. She had Independent Labour Party and Communist councillors. During World War I, her womenfolk had waged a determined (and successful) rent-strike against rapacious landlords. David Kirkwood – by 1941, the town's veteran MP – had, as an earnest and vocal pacifist, been locked up in Edinburgh Castle during that conflict and, in 1919, unrest was such that the Coalition government even sent troops and tanks into the streets of Glasgow.

In fact these "agitators" were a decent and remarkably conservative bunch; most, for instance, regularly attended church. But, in distant London, shattered Clydebank was viewed as a tinderbox of Bolshevism – especially as, at the time of the raids, there had been a protracted strike of apprentices in the local shipyards. (Not, in fact, greedy young lads, but time-served tradesmen still, unjustly, on apprentices' wages.)

On all these counts, then, officialdom toiled tirelessly to block from wider national consciousness the effective destruction of an entire community.

It is only fair to remind ourselves – seven decades later, in a comfortable age – that Britain in March 1941 was battling for national survival – bombarded from the air,

ABOVE: Evacuees in Whitecrook Street, Clydebank, wrap up from the cold after a night of heavy bombardment from the Germans

Credit: West Dunbartonshire Libraries and Cultural Services

throttled in the Atlantic, close to starving and in real fear of invasion and conquest.

The desperate desire to maintain morale, deny useful information to the foe and stamp on defeatism was by no means dishonourable. And the public information films and perky propaganda posters of the struggle are maddening today less for their bossiness than for their sexism. All the same, the fatuity of wartime censorship and propaganda – much of it to mask incompetence – is remarkable.

Churchill himself intervened in two grave misjudgements. The first was in the wake of the Dunkirk disaster, when the Ministry of Information urged folk to report "defeatists" – having established it as an offence in law to spread "alarm and despondency". Some 70 people were prosecuted after being shopped by ministry spies (cynically →

→ dubbed "Cooper's Snoopers" after the Minister of Information Duff Cooper) until Churchill ordered the nonsense to stop.

The second was after Buckingham Palace was bombed on 12 September 1940, when the King and Queen only narrowly escaped death. "The Ministry of Information, with its genius for missing propaganda opportunities," notes Lewis, "was busy suppressing news of the palace bombing when Churchill heard of it. 'Dolts, idiots, fools!' he is said to have exploded. 'Spread the news at once. Let it be broadcast everywhere.

And, when one survivor, Thomas Kearns, wrote a detailed letter to family in Belfast, it was intercepted (and held) by censors. Mr Kearns's words would not see publication till 1971

Let the people of London know that the King and Queen are sharing the perils with them...'"

Royalty was one matter; the people of Clydebank another. Whatever the motives and by whatever authority – perhaps even that of the prime minister himself – "official estimates of the damage and dead were deliberately played down", as Meg Henderson, whose novel The Holy City is based on the experience of wartime Clydebank, put it in 1999.

"Unlike modern conflicts... there were no TV cameras to bring the horror directly into the nation's living-rooms, but there were newsreel cameras. What Clydebank has never understood is why in Coventry and London the newsreel films were widely broadcast with proud boasts of 'We can take it', while in Clydebank the official view was that there had been little damage and few casualties..."

The town was never properly rebuilt; most of its March 1941 citizens never returned; and by the mid-1980s Clydebank had lost almost all her traditional industry. It's a ragged, palpably sad place today, and with one lingering legacy from past shipbuilding glory – leading all Europe in asbestos-related illness and death. ☒

John MacLeod has worked in newspapers since graduating from Edinburgh University, including as a columnist and writer-at-large for The Scotsman and The Herald. From 2002 he has written a column for the Scottish Daily Mail. He is the author of River of Fire: The Clydebank Blitz (2010)

Loose talk

43(1): 61/65 | DOI: 10.1177/0306422014522380

The Balkans has a long history of media manipulation in times of conflict. Former psychological warfare expert **Calin Hentea** gives a sometimes contentious view of the region's history, starting from the beginning of the twentieth century

FOR MANY CENTURIES the Balkan region was the battleground for three empires, Habsburg, Russian and Ottoman, and their respective faiths, Catholic, Orthodox and Islam. Until the end of the twentieth century, there was violent competition for power and influence, exacerbated by sometimes vicious rivalry between the large number of different ethnic groups. From the bloody struggles for independence from the Ottoman empire in the nineteenth century to the Kosovo war of 1999, propaganda and self-censorship played a crucial role. After the wars for independence against the Ottomans, there were conflicts over territory among the states that emerged out of the Ottoman empire. In 1912, Serbia, Bulgaria, Montenegro and Greece were victorious against Turkey, conquering multi-ethnic Macedonia. But in 1913, Bulgaria, extremely dissatisfied with its spoils from the war, attacked its former allies Serbia and Greece. To prevent the rise of an aggressive Great Bulgaria, Romanian armed forces crossed the Danube, annexing the south of Dobrodja, imposing a peace treaty on Sofia and settling the first round of the Balkan wars. But peace did not last long. Other national rivalries and antipathies grew in the hearts and minds of Balkan people – and were in part responsible for the alliances that played an important part in World War I and World War II.

As the Cold War ended, the geo-political conditions for the implosion of the Socialist Federal Republic of Yugoslavia, which had been built and sustained by Josip Broz Tito, were set in motion. His death in 1980 posed a significant threat to the narrative of the republic that Tito had so successfully championed.

In 1991, Slovenia and Croatia fought and won new wars for independence against Serbia. But the international community was unable to stop the bloody civil Bosnian war from 1992 to 1995: Bosnians, Croats and Serbs bombed, tortured, raped and killed one another, each group supported by various foreign powers.

In each conflict, individual countries used propaganda to garner political, military and economic support from dominant international powers, the foreign policy of which was consistent with its own interest.

On the eve of World War I, Serbians and Romanians asked France, Bulgaria, Turkey, the United Kingdom, Greece and Germany to support their objectives. So all state media-led propaganda was aimed at the international community, and primarily targeted Western countries. →

ABOVE: Serbian propaganda against Bulgaria following World War I

Credit: Le Petit Journal

→ As Bulgarian historian Ivan Ilcev noted in his book My Fatherland: Right or Not, which focused on Balkan propaganda aimed outside the former Yugoslavia, this continued a long-established practice dating back to the nineteenth century. In the run-up to World War I, many Balkan diplomats bribed Western journalists or officials to publish stories that supported and promoted their causes.

In order to maintain his power, Milosevic imposed tough censorship on all Serbian media

In June 1913, a year before British, French and German generals prohibited Western war correspondents from having access to the frontline, Romanian journalists were among the regiments that were advancing towards the Bulgarian capital. There was no doubt about their enthusiastic and "patriotic" coverage. Self-censorship was adopted by a huge majority of the media (with the exception of some marginal socialist journals). For example, the Romanian media dared not report on the serious number of cholera casualties among the troops, as well as the fact that the wagon that carried bread to the frontline also brought the corpses back to the homeland. Across the region, journalists and politicians were united in their attempt to hide economic conditions, poverty, corruption, and shortfalls in education, obsessed with emphasising how thoroughly the country in question was a solid part of European civilisation.

During the wars of the 1990s across the former Yugoslavia, the Balkan states alliances changed to an extent, in line with new national interests: Russia, Belarus, China and Iraq gave political support to Milosevic against NATO and the US; Croatia and Slovenia were supported by Germany; while Romania and Bulgaria had begun the process of NATO admission. Meanwhile, public opinion among Orthodox Greeks was sympathetic towards the Serbs, and Muslim Turks backed Kosovo Albanians. These alliances partly explain the different trends in how Balkan propaganda treated foreign countries during the armed conflicts of the 1990s. But Balkan public opinion was not unanimously nationalistic any more. The political opposition had grown up considerably and state media outlets within Yugoslavia presented a wide variety of attitudes and positions.

In order to maintain his power, Milosevic imposed tough censorship on all Serbian media and sought to intimidate opposition journalists through threats of enormous fines or even murder. However, Milosevic's information law, introduced on 20 October 1998, the year of the

Kosovo Liberation Army (UCK) uprising, was not the only repressive media law introduced in the region. In 1991 and 1992, during their fight for independence against the Yugoslav National Army (directed by Belgrade), the Croatian authorities imposed guidelines for state television, radio and newspapers, requiring journalists to adopt euphemistic language and coverage of any war-related issue that can only be described as propaganda, praising Croatian troops and demonising Serbian forces.

Here we come to a large common ground across the region: the demonisation of enemies and propaganda around atrocities, combined with an excess of nationalistic and patriotic rhetoric. When comparing the 1990s Balkan wars with the clashes of 1912-13, the same techniques re-appeared. In both cases, some media outlets essentially claimed that the enemy was not human, so to kill him without mercy was entirely justified and right.

The Bulgarian researcher Yura Konstantinova has written widely about the prevalence of stereotypes and prejudice in media coverage in the Balkans of 1913. The Ottoman empire was "Europe's ulcer", the Turks were cast as "Asiatic barbarians" and "a savage and uncultured tribe". By contrast, the Ottoman press characterised Bulgarian activities during the war as "atrocities, compared to which the tortures of the Inquisitions would look like true charity". Only a few months later, in 1913, the Serbs, the Greeks and the Romanians became the new Bulgarian enemies; these former allies were depicted by Mir, Sofia's semi-official newspaper, as "perfidious", "deceivers" and "allies-brigands" – meaning allies who then turned into thieves. For its part, the Romanian press labelled Bulgarians as "barbarians and conquerors", "descendants of Asparuh", referring to the Bulgarians in a pejorative way and essentially calling them uncivilised and savage. The media underlined the important duty the Romanian armed forces had to "impose civilisation" south of the Danube.

The same use of stereotypes can be traced throughout the Bosnian civil war. Peter Goff's 1999 book The Kosovo News and Propaganda War reflects first-hand impressions and analysis from important international journalists around the world about Kosovo and propaganda. As Goff points out, the Serbian media cast NATO as a "Nazi terrorist organisation"; according to newspaper Politika Ekspres, President Bill Clinton was "a liar and sexually sick person" and "a mad saxophonist Adolf Clinton", UN Secretary General Kofi Annan was "Washington's puppet", and Madeleine Albright was "the witch of our time" and "a woman with sick complexes"; the Allied air strikes were referred to as "fascist aggression".

In the run-up to World War I, many Balkan diplomats bribed Western journalists to publish stories that supported and promoted their causes

"News is the shock troops of propaganda," said the British Minister of Information Sir John Reith, in 1940. This is still valid today. Not only had the Balkan media played an important role in the international propaganda machine during wartime, Western and American media also took part and, in my opinion, often from a biased position.

Philip Knightley's book on the history of war correspondents, The First Casualty, acknowledges what most journalists know: that truth loses out in war. When it comes to war in the Balkans, whether it's the 1912-13 war or the two major armed conflicts in Bosnia and Kosovo, the truth was not entirely and honestly reflected by the media, either domestically or on an international scale. Emotional and partisan coverage, →

ABOVE: A man collects bricks in Sarajevo's main library, which was destroyed by Bosnian Serb forces in 1992

Credit: Chris Helgren/Reuters

→ combined with patriotic self-censorship on behalf of the Balkan media in 1913, was later replaced, during the three years of Bosnian civil war, with the cynical exploitation and manipulation of the international media led by individuals and groups with firm political agendas. As the award-winning BBC journalist Martin Bell acknowledged in his book In Harm's Way: "No other war – not even the Gulf war, which took on the character of a made-for-television CNN special event – has been fought so much in public, under the eye of the camera." A few years later, in spring 1999, another respected BBC correspondent John Simpson "became the direct target of the British government's public relations machine", because his reports from Belgrade under NATO bombing didn't match with Prime Minister Tony Blair's policy. It's also true that during the 1999 war, Serbian national television and the main newspapers from Belgrade acted as a perfect propaganda machine, spreading lies, prejudice and populist materials, being entirely under the power of Milosevic's guidelines and censors.

Propaganda still exists in Balkan society, and for those who report on it. All

ABOVE: A Serbian Orthodox church bombed by the Kosovo Liberation Army, 1999. The author, Calin Hentea, is on the left

of the Balkan wars of the twentieth century were sometimes poorly reported, without respect for truth, moral limits or professional ethics. Political leaders used various forms of propaganda and censorship, leading to media rhetoric. To return to the moral aphorism observed by Richard Tait, editor-in-chief of ITN, at the end of the Balkan wars: "Reporting war is too serious to be left to propagandists". ☒

Calin Hentea is a writer, academic and documentary maker. He is the author of Balkan Propaganda Wars, and served in the Romanian Armed Forces, working as an editor and officer in the force's media department. He worked extensively as a specialist with the psychological operations unit and participated in several NATO-led international missions, including to Kosovo and Afghanistan

ABOVE: Student demonstrators at Johannesburg's Witwatersrand University flee as police fired tear gas at them during an anti-apartheid protest rally in Johannesburg, South Africa August 31, 1989.

Credit: Ulli Michel/Reuters

Radio wars

43(1): 66/73 | DOI: 10.1177/0306422014522934

The long battle over white rule in South Africa and its hinterland in the second half of the twentieth century was not just a matter of military conflict, popular movements, state oppression and economic sanctions. It was also a radio propaganda war. **Keith Somerville** tells the story from both sides

LAUNCHING RADIO RSA, the external service of the South African Broadcasting Corporation (SABC), on 27 October 1965, Prime Minister Hendrick Verwoerd said it would allow "South Africa's good work to become known throughout the world". Opening the transmitters to enable apartheid South Africa to broadcast to Africa, North America, Europe, Australasia and Asia, he painted a picture of a misunderstood country seething with goodwill, and intent on building a new style of society based on separate development of the races.

Throughout the apartheid era, the official media inside the country and broadcasts transmitted externally sought to present the apartheid system as more sinned against than sinning, as a bulwark against communism and protector of Christian civilisation. Apartheid was portrayed as a brave experiment that would prevent racial conflict through segregation. Every effort was made to present white hegemony and black →

→ subordination in a positive light domestically and abroad; to denigrate African governments and black political movements; and to present the South African government as the dependable ally of the West against the Soviet bloc and China.

South Africa's version of events at home and in southern Africa did not go unchallenged. Independent African states supported the liberation movements in South Africa, Namibia, Rhodesia/Zimbabwe, Angola and Mozambique. They gave airtime on their radio services to broadcasters from liberation movements. The liberation struggle was also a propaganda war.

The thrust of South African propaganda was to play up the threat of the Soviet Union to the West and to seize on the failings of African governments

South Africa had the strongest and most advanced economy in the region and a developed network of newspapers and public radio. The print media was owned by – and served the interests of – the white elite, denying column inches and airtime to news about the black majority. Although a few publications, such as Drum magazine, were able for a while in the 1950s and early 1960s to give space to such African writers as Can Themba and Richard Rive, and although a few liberal or left-wing publications struggled to report news accurately and to represent opinions other than those of the ruling elite, the dominant media discourse was of support for white hegemony.

Before the Afrikaner National Party election victory in 1948, the media was dominated by English language newspapers owned or strongly influenced by powerful mining companies such as Anglo-American. The Afrikaans press took off after 1948. It had a more strongly conservative and overtly nationalist and racial focus than the English press. Across the mainstream press there was a broad consensus on racial segregation as well as widespread self-censorship and obedience to the commercial interests of those who owned the papers. The more liberal members of the elite – and some papers, such as the Rand Daily Mail – expressed distaste for the crudity of apartheid but few criticised it root-and-branch. The white population was the target readership for the press and, particularly after the institutionalisation of apartheid and the extension of political and economic segregation, it was fed a diet of news and comment that set the agenda for acceptance of separate development and the suppression of non-white demands for equal rights.

The SABC was a key part of the agenda-setting. Established in 1936, it was modelled closely on the BBC. At first it broadcast only in English and Afrikaans and was not set up to serve the black majority in any way. It started broadcasting in African languages in 1949, by which time it was very obviously a tool for the entrenching separate development. In that year Xhosa, Zulu and Sotho services were broadcast on shortwave. In 1960 the services were expanded but moved to FM, and cheap FM sets flooded the market to discourage short-wave listening, as this would, in the National Party's view, lead to black South Africans hearing broadcasts from independent states, such as Ghana and Egypt, advocating an end to white minority rule in southern Africa. The SABC under the National Party regime was closely linked to the elite Broederbond organisation that was at the heart of Afrikaner political, economic, cultural and military dominance. The SABC was wholly committed to supporting the development of apartheid and the use of the media to promote it and drown out any dissenting voices.

Under apartheid, the media were used to attack aggressively even the mildest critics of the regime, to advance the arguments for apartheid as a system of government at home and abroad, and to press the case for western support for the survival of a white South Africa as a defence against communism and its radical African nationalist allies. One key tactic, as described by John Laurence, a former propagandist with the South African Department of Information, in his 1968 book The Seeds of Disaster, was to project a view of "injured innocence" in the face of accusations of racism and brutality, and to describe South Africa as "a benevolent Christian state, faced with unique racial problems and earnestly and even generously doing its best to solve them in a manner which will prove fair and just to all concerned". This would be a constant theme of South African propaganda as broadcast through SABC and its external services and encouraged in newspapers.

The dominance of the National Party-run state over the broadcast media, along with government control of and heavy self-censorship by the commercial print media, ensured a consistent message was given to South Africans that there really was no alternative – that white support of the system and acquiescence by everyone else was the only viable course. Liberation movements and dissenting voices were vilified or not reported. When what remained of the liberal press tried to step outside the parameters of allowable reporting or comment, journalists faced harassment and legal action under a panoply of laws. After Donald Woods, editor of the Rand Daily Mail, championed the cause of Black Consciousness leader Steve Biko and demanded an investigation into his death in 1977, he was forced to flee the country in fear of his life. The Rand Daily Mail correspondent Ben Pogrund was subject to relentless persecution for nearly 30 years.

Direct censorship was used by the National Party when self-censorship didn't work. The Suppression of Communism Act of 1950 prevented certain people being quoted by the media and criminalised the African National Congress (ANC) and the

ABOVE: Oliver Tambo, president of the African National Congress addresses a crowd of 15,000 supporters at a Free Nelson Mandela rally

Credit: PA/PA Archive/Press Association Images

Pan-Africanist Congress (PAC). During the state of emergency period in the mid-1980s, reporting of political violence and internal civil movements was severely curtailed. There were constraints even on what could be said about poverty and deprivation in the black community. Propaganda, or "telling our side of the story" as one senior NP politician, Adriaan Vlok, told me in 1990, was a valuable and consistently used tool for developing and protecting apartheid within South Africa.

The launch of regime-run Radio RSA in 1965 was a response to a growing →

→ number of African states achieving independence, declaring their enthusiastic support for the ANC and the PAC and allowing southern African liberation groups to broadcast from their radio stations. Regular broadcasts giving an African nationalist version of the news and relaying speeches or commentaries from such leaders as Oliver Tambo attacking apartheid were heard in South Africa. The South African regime decided that it had to broadcast its version of events to Africa and counter opposition to apartheid across the world. Radio RSA was expanded rapidly from 1965 to cover the whole of Africa in a variety of languages – initially English, French, Portuguese and Afrikaans, but later also Nyanja, Zulu, Swahili, German and Spanish.

What the ANC was trying to encourage through Radio Freedom was not hatred against whites in general but a broadening of the resistance to apartheid

I monitored South African domestic and external radio for the BBC Monitoring Service in the early 1980s and edited transcripts from South Africa and the ANC's Radio Freedom from 1983 until late 1988. The thrust of South African external propaganda was to play up the threat of the Soviet Union to the West and to Africa, to seize on any example of the failings of African governments, of conflicts, coups and corruption, to try to undermine domestic support for those governments and to portray the liberation movements as a threat to Africa. News was carefully selected and angled to give the worst possible picture of such African leaders as Kenneth Kaunda and Julius Nyerere and to run down Western critics. Governments and people in target areas, such as

Apartheid: A journalist's story

Natasha Joseph interviews her father, a journalist in South Africa during apartheid, about how the state tried to pump propaganda through the newspapers

One Saturday, sometime during the late 1970s or early 1980s, police officers raided the South Africa Sunday Times' offices. It was a blessing in disguise for Joe Sutton, then news editor of the influential weekly: until the officers burst into his newsroom, he had been scrambling to find a lead story. Sutton called his photographic team from their office upstairs and commissioned pictures. Just like that, the Sunday Times had a page one lead.

Raymond Joseph is laughing as he tells me the story. Yes, Joseph is my father - and, like me, he's a journalist. I, however, came of age as a reporter after democracy, taking up my first full-time newsroom job in 2000 when I was 19. My dad started out as a cub reporter in 1974 and worked for The Rand Daily Mail, the Sunday Express and the Sunday Times.

As a junior, I battled to develop contacts and refine my nose for stories. When he was a junior, my dad was trying to figure out which of his colleagues were spies working for the apartheid government and the vicious security police. "The spooks were very good. You knew there were spies in the newsroom, and it was a situation where you eyed people around the room and no one trusted anyone. You were very careful. There was a guy called Gordon Winter - he turned out to be spying for (the Bureau of State Security) BOSS. His handler, Hendrick van den Bergh, was head of BOSS.

"As a young reporter, the system we had at the Express was that every junior was assigned to a senior as a mentor. Winter was mine. He taught me a lot of good stuff. "He knew that stories were being planted, but the role of reporters like Winter and other spooks was to find others to do the writing so the "obvious people" wouldn't have their names associated with pro-government stories.

This sowed a great deal of mistrust in South African newsrooms, which worked in the government's favour as it made journalists extremely cautious and led to self-censorship that was often as tough as the draconian rules imposed by the apartheid state. "You never really knew where a story was coming from. We knew that sources used us, but we used sources... and as long as you can begin to understand how you're being used..." he trails off.

To avoid being fooled, he, and other journalists, used the basic tricks of the trade: multiple sources, thorough double- and triple-checking. "As a news editor during the states of emergency (in the late 1980s), I can remember a time when the South African Sunday Times carried on its front page week after week after week, a warning to readers to 'be aware that what you're reading in this newspaper may not be the entire story'. Newspapers were never censored. (The government) passed draconian laws with serious implications so you were self-censoring."

Nowhere was this clearer than in a handy little legal guide for South African reporters called The Newspaperman's Guide to the Law. Dad has all three editions. The first, published in 1968, was "a thin little book which had just more than 100 pages". The second edition came out in 1977, it was 302 pages. The third ran to 410 pages.

"There were constantly new laws, some of which are still on the statute books in South Africa today. Under the Police Act, if you published something about the police, you must have taken reasonable steps to prove it was true... in this case, the way to do that was to ask the police, who would deny it. So if you published in the face of a denial, you were breaking the law."

"You were constantly approached, being offered money to work for the police - it happened to me as a young journalist. The conventional wisdom was that if you accept money, they only have to pay you once, because then they can blackmail you."

Once approached, a journalist who wanted to stay clean would go straight to their editor or news editor to report it so it "couldn't be held against you."

"Those were strange days and the apartheid government was very successful, because you never felt you could trust the person in the desk next to you. You didn't know who was saying yes."

Natasha Joseph is news editor at City Press, Johannesburg

Zambia and Tanzania, were aware of these broadcasts but evidence from interviews with radio listeners in Dar es Salaam and Arusha in 1986 and 1988 and later in Zambia in 1991 did not indicate a wide listenership or a massive effect. Kaunda told me in 1991 that he was more concerned about economic destabilisation and direct attacks or infiltration of South African agents than what was said by Radio RSA.

South Africa also sought to influence events in southern Africa by funding and providing technical assistance and transmitters for the radio stations of the pro-western National Union for the Total Independence of Angola guerrilla army, Voice of the Resistance of the Black Cockerel, and Renamo in Mozambique. These had more effect because of the civil wars in those countries, the existence of rebel-held areas with large populations and a level of opposition to governments resulting from poverty and conflict.

The ANC's first brief foray into radio propaganda was in June 1963 – three years after the banning of the ANC in the wake of the Sharpeville massacre. A station calling itself Freedom Radio was broadcast from Lilliesleaf Farm in Rivonia, the covert base for the underground ANC and South African Communist Party (SACP). The station lasted weeks before the police raid on the farm led to the imprisonment of most of the internal leadership of the ANC-SACP alliance.

The ANC broadcasts then relied on transmitters and airtime provided by Egypt, Tanzania and Zambia to get messages across. The external services of these countries transmitted regular ANC broadcasts and were later joined by Angola, Mozambique, Ethiopia and Madagascar. By 1965, Dar es Salaam Radio was broadcasting material on behalf of the ANC. Radio Freedom itself started in 1967 with transmission from Zambia. Broadcasts were intermittent but became regular from Dar es Salaam and Lusaka by 1969. Programmes were →

ABOVE: A local newspaper billboard proclaims the Commonwealth decision to give South Africa a six-month deadline to dismantle apartheid before major economic sanctions are introduced, in Johannesburg, October 1985

→ broadcast to South Africa in English, Tswana, Zulu, Xhosa, Sotho and Afrikaans.

Before the Soweto uprising in 1976 and the drawn-out domestic resistance by the United Democratic Front, the Confederation of South African Trade Unions and other movements in the 1980s, the broad thrust of Radio Freedom was to tell black South Africans that the ANC still existed, to broadcast messages from Oliver Tambo, Thabo Mbeki and other leaders, and to call for support for liberation. Its impact was limited by shortages of short-wave sets, by government attempts to block broadcasts and by the failure of the ANC to launch a credible armed struggle inside South Africa. Soweto was a turning point. ANC radio and other propaganda – often spread by word of mouth or through group listening to radio – assured black youth activists that the ANC still existed and supported them. Around 4,000 young black South Africans left the country between June 1976 and early 1977, the majority to join the ANC and get military training.

But it was in the 1980s – particularly after the declaration of the state of emergency on 20 July 1985 in areas of the Eastern Cape, the PWV region (Pretoria, Witwatersrand and Vereeniging) and later in parts of the Western Cape – that Radio Freedom became particularly influential. During the emergency period, SABC became a key instrument for the government, with increasing restrictions on the commercial press. Radio Freedom was increasingly important at this time even though relatively few people had short-wave radios and listening was banned by the government. The United Democratic Front (UDF) activist Raymond Suttner, a member of the ANC and the SACP, recently told me that groups of activists would gather to listen to broadcasts. The UDF activist Murphy Morobe, a former student leader, has said that even when little of the content of the broadcast could be heard, the sound of Radio Freedom, with a burst of machinegun fire in its opening station ident, was enough to give encouragement. Suttner believes the numbers listening were low and "these had to be small groups or individuals on their own because it was illegal. So it cannot be quantified. It had quite a lot of influence... during the 1985-86 state of emergency, we in the UDF were guided by some of the broadcasts, especially on negotiations and popular power." Perhaps as little as 1 per cent of the population listened, but leaders of the domestic protest movements tuned in and messages from the ANC spread by word of mouth.

The most controversial aspect, and one brought up recently in the debate in South Africa over former ANC Youth League

Credit: Greg English/AP/Press Association Images

leader Julius Malema's public singing of the liberation war song "Shoot the Boer", is the extent to which Radio Freedom promoted hatred of whites, Afrikaners in particular.

The writer James Myburgh has suggested that the radio was propagating a message of hate through its encouragement of attacks in rural areas and the planting of landmines. He quotes a Radio Freedom broadcast from Addis Ababa on 28 November 1985 in which the ANC took credit for planting landmines, saying that this was a "sign of the intensification of the struggle" and that for white South Africans this would soon "become the order of the day". In February 1986, Chris Hani, the political commissar and deputy head of Umkhonto we Sizwe (MK), the ANC's armed wing, broadcast that white farmers were part of the apartheid rural security network and economy and were legitimate targets. Hani stressed that MK was not targeting white civilians indiscriminately or because of their race.

A closer analysis of Radio Freedom broadcasts shows a consistent policy of stressing – in broadcasts by Hani, by SACP and MK leader Joe Slovo and others – a clear delineation between "legitimate targets" and the white population in general. A broadcast in July 1987 included a recording of Hani saying: "It's not a racial war...the country is in a state of civil war... We must go for installations in the white areas. We are already going for the farmers, because the farmers are an important element of the South African Defence Force."

What the ANC was trying to encourage through Radio Freedom was not hatred against whites in general but a broadening of the resistance to apartheid, setting an agenda of broad support for the armed struggle and warning white South Africans that they would not have a secure future under apartheid.

Radio Freedom was an instrument of liberation propaganda, strongly supported the armed struggle and was vehemently anti-apartheid but not anti-white. Neither it nor the SABC and Radio RSA spread overt messages of hate or incitement to hatred – they were about propaganda. The difference was that SABC and RSA were covertly propagandistic to support a system of racial hegemony through the broadcast of slanted and very narrow news and comment, while Radio Freedom was overtly an organ of propaganda seeking to advance the ANC's struggle. ☒

Keith Somerville is a senior research fellow at the Institute of Commonwealth Studies, University of London; teaches in the School of Politics and International Relations and the Centre for Journalism at the University of Kent; and edits the Africa news and analysis website www.africajournalismtheworld.com

Political vacuum opens up propaganda possibilities

43(1): 74/77 | DOI: 10.1177/0306422014523379

Now we no longer trust politicians, we are more open to believing propoganda from other sources, argues **Max Wind-Cowie**

THE FIRST CASUALTY of war is the truth. So said, well... lots of people actually. So many people that I really didn't want to start this article with it. It's a cliché. Such a ubiquitous and timeless expression of cynicism that no one can even agree on who said it first – the candidates including an Ancient Greek playwright, a long-dead US Senator and Samuel Johnson. But just as politicians, essayists and satirists throughout the ages have kept coming back to it, so in the end, did I. Because, like so many clichés, it is a simple and transparent truism. The reality is that when the stakes are as high as they surely must always be in warfare, lying and misleading and emitting and embellishing are all just too tempting to be resisted. Propaganda, in short, will always find a space in the nooks and crannies of battle.

The two world wars offer a master-class in how governments can sustain public consent to self-sacrifice

It is easy to understand why propaganda matters in war. The sacrifices and burdens that war places on the citizenry – from rationing to mass bereavement to the fear of imminent destruction – can be excruciating. The consequences of apathy amongst your soldiers can be devastating. The benefits of winning over as-yet ambivalent or neutral governments and peoples to your cause can be decisive. All of these audiences require encouragement, reinforcement and persuasion – and that's before one even gets to the possibilities contained in convincing one's enemy of the futility or injustice of their own cause.

The two great conflicts of the twentieth century, World War I, whose centenary we commemorate and mourn this year, and World War II, which ended 69 years ago, witnessed huge innovation and investment in the strange art of propaganda.

These efforts succeeded in mobilising 65 million active combatants in World War I and nearly 100 million in the second. What is more, propaganda played a huge role in keeping the home fronts of countries on both sides on board with these gargantuan

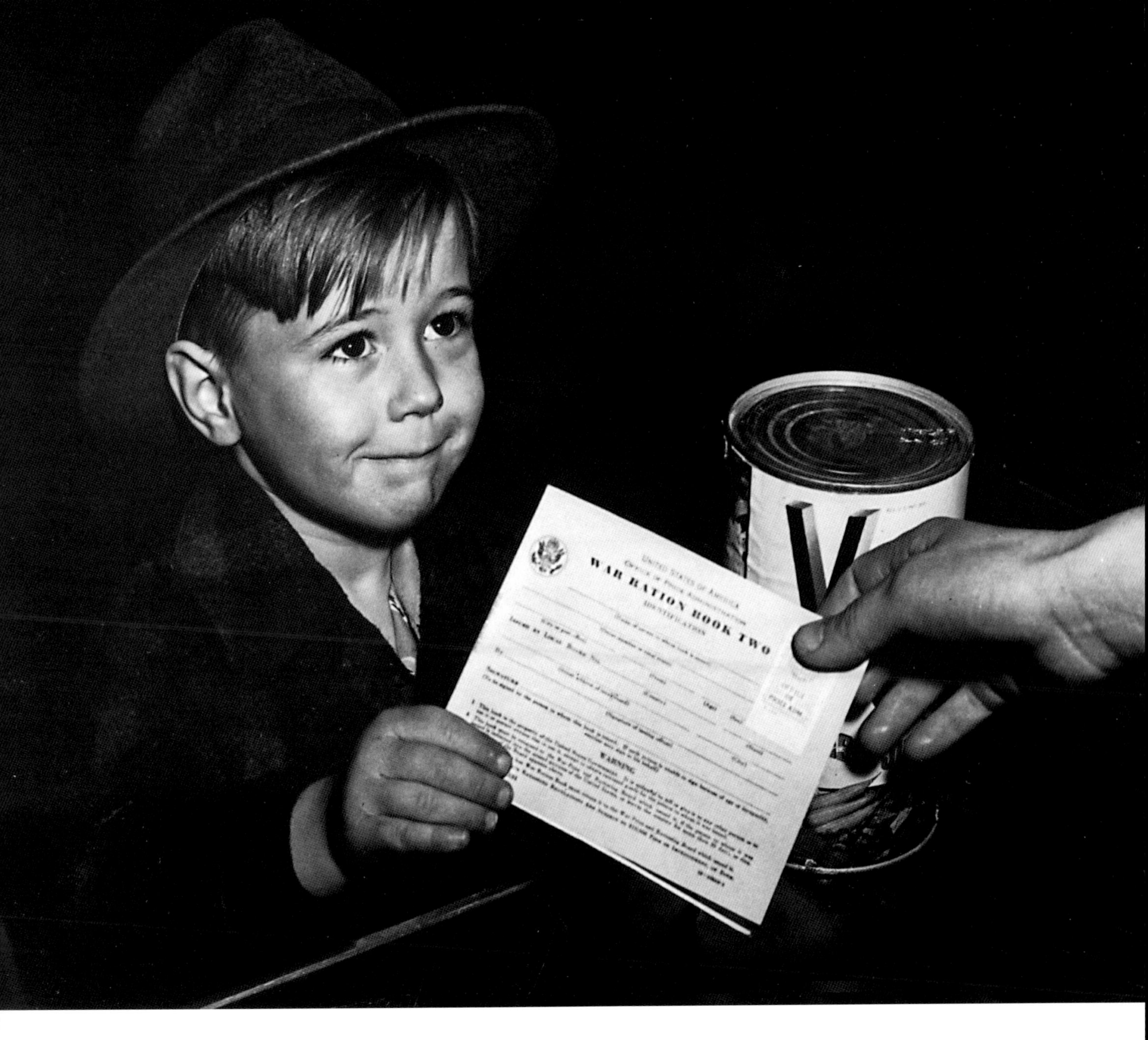

ABOVE: A child collects food with a ration book during World War II

Credit: MPVHistory / Alamy

exercises in total conflict. In the UK in 2011 riots on the streets of London were widely diagnosed as symptoms of welfare reform – the people saw a benefits cap of £26,000 a year looming and took to the streets. During World War II British citizens were restricted by government edict to measly weekly allocations of meat, tea, jam, biscuits, breakfast cereals, cheese, eggs, lard, milk and canned and dried fruit. They did not smash up central London in outrage – partly because the Germans were doing that for them but mostly because the majority was sufficiently convinced of the necessity of their suffering.

The two world wars offer a master-class in how governments can sustain public consent to self-sacrifice. The British government spent much of World War I mixing fear and outrage into a potent and highly effective mood enhancer for the British people. Tall tales of German barbarism were told – in exercises straight out of the "atrocity propaganda" playbook – in order both to inspire a humanitarian urge to intervention and to remind voters of the consequences of defeat for themselves and their families. The Ministry of Information (which Western government would dare such a name in our post-Orwell world?) pumped out literature, press releases, movies and posters – much of →

→ them balancing a narrative of British pluck with Germanic inhumanity.

The classic of the genre remains the Bryce Report on German "war crimes" which brilliantly and vividly terrified the public of Britain and America with its depiction of the systematic rape, mutilation, murder and cannibalism deployed by German soldiers on Belgian civilians. It was bone-chilling stuff for British people who, when it was published in 1915, were also subject to constant warnings from their government that invasion by the Germans was a real and present danger. This work of – at the very least – exaggeration was also transformative when

Tall tales of German barbarism were told – in exercises straight out of the "atrocity propaganda" playbook – in order both to inspire a humanitarian urge to intervention

it came to American public opinion. Hot on the heels of the Germans' sinking of a ship sailing from New York to the UK, the Bryce Report gained sensational coverage in the US and helped swing America into action.

How true the accusations in the Bryce Report were remains a bone of some considerable contention. A significant percentage of the witness statements describing the mass-brutalisation of Belgium by German troops came from defeated Belgian soldiers – and many historians and scholars argue that the Bryce Report hugely inflated the systemic nature of German barbarism and the level of deliberate suffering imposed on the Belgian civilian population. But whatever its questionable worth as a historic document, the Bryce Report was gold dust for the whizz kids at the Ministry of Information – who ensured sensationalist headlines at home and abroad, depicted German soldiers bayonetting children in posters and reminded, none-too-subtly, British mums and dads that should we lose, this would be the fate of little Jimmy and Sally too.

There is no real point in arguing about the ethics of using the faults of one's enemies – often grotesquely exaggerated faults – to win and to keep support. It is, when the stakes are so high, an inevitable temptation. And the Germans were at it too – producing some of the most ludicrous scare stories about British troops ever to grace the written word. But the point I am trying to make is that, back then, it was effective – supremely so at times. But it just isn't effective anymore.

The world of 1915 is gone forever. It is impossible now to imagine a government in the democratic world able to wield so much influence over the mind-sets, hopes, fears and beliefs of their public with such ease. The Bryce Report was a shaky dossier of dodgy evidence sexed up to suit the cause of war. And on the whole, folk bought it. Coverage was blanket and was emphatic in its faith in the conclusions of the government – for millions in the UK in 1915 it simply became the truth that German soldiers bayonetted and, perhaps, ate children. Compare that with 2003, when the government released a report on another despotic regime intent on regional domination. That document too was, at best, unreliable in its sourcing and heavy on the red alert messaging. It, too, was a small part of a larger case for standing up to tyranny – one that was perhaps a tad over the top about the imminent terror the enemy represented. But the infamous "dodgy dossier" that formed part of Prime Minister Blair's justification for invading Iraq was mocked and monstered almost from the start.

Allegation and innuendo about how the "dodgy dossier" had been constructed meant that, even as Blair won his vote on intervention, the British public were already closing their ears. It's hard to win a propaganda war when your public won't even listen to your elegant reconstruction of the truth.

That's not to say that Blair was undone by some particular "crime" committed by him or his staff. But rather, it is to point to a sad but surely unarguable truth – we're just more cynical about government communication now. We're more sophisticated. We have access to a myriad of alternative sources of comment and analysis – for better or for worse – and we presume our politicians are lying to us all the live long day. Only 18 per cent of the British public trust politicians to tell the truth. Which means that when a government minister starts trying to tell us that there's a big bad wolf at the door, 82 in every 100 of us is already turning to our neighbour and saying, "he's probably making this up you know".

And there's another factor at play here. Because we no longer believe what our governments tell us we are left open and available to misinformation and disinformation from other sources instead. Propaganda hasn't died as we've become less credulous of our political class – it has blossomed. But the propagandists now live entirely outside any pretence of democratic accountability. NGOs, lobby groups, corporations and media outfits funded and controlled by foreign governments but with a mask of independence, compete to convince us – on questions of war and peace more than on almost anything else. Whether these organisations represent a Dovish point of view or a Hawkish one is besides the point – what matters is that they fill the vacuum created by our mistrust in our politics and our governments. And they can say whatever they want because we no longer have any mutually agreed base line of impartiality.

So it is that Iraq Body Count could say in 2006 that 50,000 Iraqi civilians had died in Operation Enduring Freedom and its aftermath, while The Lancet said it was over half a million. A host of interventionist lobby groups claim it was far fewer than either. In a 2008 poll more British people agreed that the invasion of Iraq was "to gain control of Iraq's oil" than signed up to any other rationale. In the absence of a trusted government to tell us stories about why we go to war there is instead a free-for-all fog of conspiracy theories, lies, third-party propaganda and outright fantasy. All competing for our attention. All drowning out the enfeebled voices of our leaders.

I know that many will shout "hurray". A competition of voices, ideas and explanations can surely only be a good thing? Well yes – to a point. And of course it is not necessarily better to have a government that lies to you than to have an NGO or a pressure group do the same. But here's the thing. When I think of the sacrifices that were made by the everyday man and woman in order to defeat German domination in World War I, and the plague of Nazism in World War II, I am – like many people – moved. Together, millions sacrificed themselves – flesh, freedom, food and so much more – in order to accomplish great things that were only truly achievable through war. It might not be fashionable or reassuring to say so but there are some evils that can only be triumphed against by use of force and by mass suffering. In a democracy consent needs to be won in order for these things to be doable. We have to volunteer to suffer. And in the absence of a political elite capable of inspiring us to believe their propaganda over the hubbub of everyone else's, I think we have good cause to be frightened that we shall never again be able or willing to stand up and be counted as once we were. ☒

Max Wind-Cowie is a writer, political consultant and an associate of the think-tank Demos

Holding the line

43(1): 78/81 | DOI: 10.1177/0306422014522167

News coverage has changed dramatically since World War I, and how the military handles it has changed too. **Major Ric Cole**, a serving army officer, gives his perspective on how the relationship between the media and military works

IN 1914, NEWS from the frontline took weeks, even months, to reach home. Or at least to reach those in power, who then decided what news was propagated to the general public and how. News was then disseminated across garden fences, in pubs and in churches. The death of a local lad was a bitter shock to those who knew him and his village and community grieved for him. Those names are still recorded on war memorials up and down the country.

During World War II, Alan Wicker and the teams from the Army Film and Photographic Unit (AFPU) were recruited from film studios and travelled with combat units capturing actions in North Africa to Italy, and from Normandy to Paris and Berlin. These news reels played in cinemas across the country, informing the population and motivating them to support the war effort.

Times were different by the early 1970s after the tide of US public opinion turned against the war in Vietnam which had been playing out on TVs and in the papers for several years. It was the returning veterans who felt despised by those who believed the war was wrong and betrayed by a government keen to wash its hands of a failed campaign in a far-away land.

By 1991, the world had changed and the liberation of Kuwait from Iraqi occupation during Operation Desert Storm was the first conflict to be broadcast live. BBC and CNN reporters witnessed Tomahawk cruise missiles, fired from US warships far out in the Arabian Gulf, passing their hotel windows. The media, gathered in Saudi Arabia, were pooled to ensure that all outlets were given the same stories to broadcast and the US commander, General Norman Schwarzkopf gave regular and frequent press conferences, during which videos of precision strikes were played. This was a new kind of warfare, played out on televisions and radios across the world.

After 1991, the British Ministry of Defence (MoD) looked long and hard at how better to conduct media operations, wondering how, and if, a military force could ensure that the stories in the world's media accurately reflected its operational business.

In current UK MoD publications, media operations are defined as: "That line of activity developed to ensure timely, accurate and effective provision [through the media] of public information and implementation of public relations (PR) policy within the operational environment whilst maintaining Operational Security (OPSEC)."

First, the MoD established the Defence Media Operations Centre (DMOC). DMOC has two key roles: to train press officers at

ABOVE: A BBC television crew reports from the front line of Ivory Coast's main city Abidjan in April, 2011. Forces loyal to Ivory Coast incumbent leader Laurent Gbagbo stepped up a counter-attack on presidential claimant Alassane Ouattara by firing on his hotel headquarters in Abidjan

Credit: Emmanuel Braun/Reuters

all levels and to deploy, at short notice, media teams to cover events involving the UK military.

Furthermore, the tradition of Wicker's AFPU continues through the use of combat camera teams, which are deployed with battlefield units to capture full-motion high-definition video and still images of combat in situations where it would be too dangerous to embed a civilian journalist. This footage is then distributed to news outlets around the world to be used for free. But what about accusations that the footage is censored? Naturally, the military will not distribute footage and imagery that make the armed forces look unprofessional, but nothing →

ABOVE: Part of a collection of rare British World War II propaganda posters sold at auction in Sussex, UK in 2010

→ is fabricated or deleted and everything is saved as part of the operational record, eventually ending up at the Imperial War

The military will not distribute footage and imagery that make the armed forces look unprofessional, but nothing is fabricated or deleted

Museum for archiving and in time, eventual disclosure to the public.

Secondly, the military recognised that by far the best way to get its message out is directly through trusted and respected media outlets. To facilitate this, the MoD Directorate of Media and Communications runs a programme which embeds reporters with combat units. Everyone from smaller regional outlets including local newspapers, to national and international broadcasters such as the BBC, ITN and Sky News are all given the opportunity to travel to the front line. They are escorted, protected, fed, transported and accommodated and given access to soldiers and commanders.

Each news organisation and reporter signs The Green Book. This formal agreement outlines what the embedded journalist can expect from the military (a bed, food, transport and the same level of protection afforded to soldiers, which includes a helmet and body armour if necessary), and in return the military reserves the right to review any copy or other output for breaches of operational security (OPSEC).

OPSEC is not about censorship and gagging. It is a constant process which aims to ensure that essential elements of friendly (ie UK or coalition) information are protected. This denies the adversary any details of troop dispositions, capabilities or intentions and in doing so saves lives (possibly including the life of the embedded journalist).

Trusted journalists are given access to military planning and are allowed to sit in as orders are given to subordinate units. This provides journalists with a richer understanding of the operation, helps them understand what the military commander is attempting to achieve and places the journalist's report in a wider context.

Recent events in the Middle East and North Africa have highlighted the power of social media. As one Egyptian protester said, "We use Facebook to schedule the protests, Twitter to coordinate, and YouTube to tell the world."

The UK MoD has engaged with this upsurge in social media and today most

Credit: Nigel Bowles/Rex Features

military units have a Facebook page. The MoD itself has thousands of followers on Twitter and all military personnel are issued guidelines for online behaviour, ensuring that the highest standards of behaviour are maintained.

Today, support for UK Armed Forces is as high as at any time in living memory. The general public have learned, unlike at the time of Vietnam, that it is possible to disagree with the war but still back the troops sent there to fight it on their behalf. Many of those soldiers, sailors and airmen are on active on social media sites and some have an astonishing number of followers.

Twenty-four hour news, mobile phones, citizen journalists, bloggers, Twitter and the internet are not going to go away and are now considered very much part of the modern battlespace, just as war is very much part of the news agenda. The enemy, the civilian population and numerous other actors have always been present in war, but they all now have a voice and a global audience.

The discipline of information operations is now at the very heart of UK military doctrine. From the presence and appearance of a soldier on patrol engaging with local communities to the perception of the armed forces in the national and international media, the information shared and what is kept safe will play a crucial role in determining the outcome of any contemporary conflict involving UK and Western forces.

Terrorist groups such as al Qaeda and al Shabab understand this and seek to dominate the information environment, with the latter tweeting live as the assault on the Westgate shopping mall in Nairobi, Kenya, was conducted. This is the enemy now faced by UK forces and as such they must be prepared to fight for information, be first with the truth and, above all, have a much better understanding of their target audiences at home and abroad. ☒

Major Ric Cole joined the UK Armed Forces in 1995. He served as a Royal Marine commando and as an infantry officer in Northern Ireland for eight years and left the regular army in 2007. As a reservist, Major Cole has served in Iraq (2008) and Afghanistan (2009) conducting media operations, and spent two years as a senior analyst with the Defence Science & Technology Laboratory. Currently assigned to the Land Warfare Centre in Warminster, Major Cole advises on and teaches information operations. He is also an MoD social media mentor, providing guidance to service personnel online @ ric_cole

Dispatches from the frontline

43(1): 82/85 | DOI: 10.1177/0306422014526122

Seasoned foreign correspondent **Lyse Doucet** discusses war reporting and how it has changed in the past 25 years

"**COVERING A WAR** means going to places torn by chaos, destruction and death, and trying to bear witness. It means trying to find the truth in a sandstorm of propaganda when armies, tribes or terrorists clash."

Those words were spoken, with conviction and clarity, by correspondent Marie Colvin when she gave an address for the war wounded at St Bride's Church in London in November 2010.

A little more than a year later, Marie was killed during an attack on a makeshift media centre in the embattled Syrian city of Homs. Her death was widely mourned by friends and fans, far and wide, who hailed her as the "bravest of the brave" war correspondent of our generation.

And her death gave many of us pause for thought on what she had called "our mission to report these horrors of war with accuracy and without prejudice".

By the end of 2013, at least 63 journalists had died on this "mission" covering the nearly three-year long war in Syria according to the Committee to Protect Journalists (CPJ). And the story does not end there. There are at least 30, possibly 40, journalists kidnapped in Syria, many of whom have disappeared without a trace. They could be alive, or dead. From what we know from those who have escaped their ordeal, or were freed, their plight is likely to be horrific.

It's this ominous threat of abduction, mainly from Islamist groups linked to al Qaeda, that has led many journalists to stop, however reluctantly, their trips into opposition-controlled areas.

With much of the reporting in the most volatile areas of Syria being done by freelancers, the growing danger led the Rory Peck Trust, an agency dedicated to freelancers' care, to issue an unprecedented statement entitled: "Do you really have to go to Syria?" It spoke of a situation that was "becoming more dangerous and unpredictable by the day".

It's long been a mantra of journalism that: "no story is worth dying for." Gone are the days when journalists felt our profession afforded us some protection. Journalists are being targeted, not just in Syria, but in conflicts everywhere from Afghanistan to Somalia to Colombia. And even in countries not at war, like Egypt, those with power take aim at the media.

But it's still said: some stories are worth taking risks for. And Syria is still one of them: one of the most punishing wars of our time; one of the gravest humanitarian crises; a conflict which draws in an entire region, and major capitals beyond. But it's the kind

ABOVE: French photographer Remi Ochlik in Cairo, Egypt, on 23 November 2011. Ochlik was killed in February 2012 in the Syrian city of Homs by government rocket fire

Credit: Julien de Rosa/Handout/Reuters

of war where you often don't know how great the risks are, until it is too late.

Friends who met Marie Colvin in Beirut as she prepared for her ill-fated assignment spoke of her unease over an unpredictable foray with smugglers into the besieged city dubbed the "capital of the revolution".

When a mutual friend, veteran correspondent Lindsey Hilsum of Channel 4 News, told Marie that trip was beyond her own threshold of danger, Marie had a simple strong reply.

"It's what we do." It's what journalists have been doing for as long as there have been wars to cover.

Just after Marie died, a Syrian diplomat admitted to me that he had repeatedly tried, and failed, to get Marie a visa so that she could enter the country legally and, in principle, more safely. It could have made all the difference.

In this war, journalists tend to divide into; those who work in areas controlled by opposition forces, those – including myself – able to obtain government visas, and journalists who have decided it's not possible to cover the story at all, given the mounting risks.

Often, sitting with colleagues in Beirut, who talk about "going in", I am →

ABOVE: Lyse Doucet on assignment in the Tadoman neighbourhood of Damascus, Syria

→ reminded of a war a quarter century ago where journalists set up shop in the Pakistani frontier cities of Peshawar and Quetta. There was that constant query: "Are you going inside?" That conflict was the war between Afghan mujahideen backed by the West and much of the Muslim world against a Soviet-backed government in Kabul.

Most journalists reporting on that war gone by also tended to cover one side or the other, partly because of the difficulty of

Journalists are being targeted, not just in Syria, but in conflicts everywhere from Afghanistan to Somalia to Colombia

getting visas for Kabul, and partly out of choice. In a Cold War era, there was a sense for some of wanting to report from what was perceived to be the right side of history.

I began reporting from Pakistan in 1988 and then obtained a visa to go to Kabul as another harsh winter closed in and Soviet troops began to pull out. Some mujahideen commanders gave me letters promising safe passage in case I entered areas under their control. There was also a warning that the end was nigh for President Najibullah's government.

A year later, when I left Kabul and returned to live in Pakistan, still hoping to continue to cover both sides, the Afghan foreign minister threatened to cut off contact because I had "gone over to the enemy". But the threat never materialised and I still travelled back and forth. "Hospitality over ideology" prevailed among most Afghans.

But it was also a time of danger, on all sides of this war. This meant death threats to journalists, including the BBC, the murder of a few colleagues, and the risks which come from covering any violent confrontation. Each life lost matters, and gratefully, they were fewer in number then.

We used to say then that the bravest journalist was the one who could summon up courage in front of colleagues to say "no" – no to boarding a Soviet military helicopter or embarking on a road trip fraught with risk, even if a lot of other journalists decided to go, no matter what.

That was a time before Twitter, email, or even proper phone systems. Kabul had only two international telephone lines on their exchange. One, for some reason, went through Glasgow, and the operators there became my daily companions down a crackling, and no doubt heavily bugged, line. Queues formed of journalists, fretting over deadlines, next to the few teletype machines that clattered away, night and day, in gloomy hotel lobbies.

In contrast in Syria today, journalists have the ability to go live with the latest technology wherever they are, safety and power sources permitting.

But use of technology may bring risks. It's alleged that the attack which killed Marie Colvin along with the talented young French photojournalist Remi Ochlik, and injured and killed others, was a targeted killing. The Syrian military is said to have picked up satellite signals used by journalists in the media house next to a makeshift clinic run by opposition forces.

In Syria, journalists are also stopped at government crossings if they have stamps from the northern border where opposition

forces hold sway. It's harder to get a visa if you have gone in from that side which the Syrian government regards as a violation of its sovereignty.

And for extreme groups on all sides, journalists can be seen as spies, symbols of western powers, or useful bargaining chips.

Most journalists now go to war zones armed with hostile environment training, including basic first aid, and advice on how to deal with an array of threats. But as the Rory Peck Trust noted: "this is a new situation where no amount of planning or preparation can reliably reduce the possibility of kidnapping or abduction."

There is another major difference in the coverage of our time. If journalists can't be there on the ground, due to dangers or difficulties, there will almost always be someone else to tell at least part of the story. We live in a time when no one can say: "I didn't know it was happening."

On social media including Twitter, Facebook and YouTube there is a constant stream of films, photographs, comment, and cries for help. Activists and engaged citizens, armed with a telephone or a computer, want their stories to be heard and don't have to wait for journalists to help them.

There is also a vast spectrum of local television channels, radio stations, and newspapers in every part of the world. This gives journalists everywhere an extraordinary array of eyewitness accounts and videos to tell stories from a distance.

But even with this unprecedented access to sources of information, there is still the age-old challenge once known as the "fog of war". Sifting facts from fiction, verifying videos, checking accounts from warring sides is still our stock in trade. Trying to find truth doesn't get easier.

I recently had reason to return to records of that earlier war a quarter of a century ago. The photographs turned back the time: children screaming in the wake of a rocket attack; long queues for petrol with Afghans shivering in winter cold; Soviet soldiers proudly standing guard; a magazine cover with President Najibullah's photograph with its bold headline "Will He Last?"

Decades on, many of us cover another punishing war, this time in Syria, where children also pay a terribly heavy price, and a Russian-backed President does battle with an array of opposition forces backed by the West.

Afghanistan's own war hasn't ended and still takes a heavy toll on civilians, including brave Afghan journalists determined to tell their own country's story.

Some things don't change about the brutality of war. And one thing will never change about journalism. Every journalist knows that feeling in the gut: when a story matters, you want to "be there."

In some ways, it's easier now to tell these stories of our time, and in other ways, far harder.

Marie Colvin's testimony still stands: "Covering a war means going to places torn by chaos, destruction and death, and trying to bear witness." ☒

Lyse Doucet is the BBC's chief international correspondent. She tweets @bbclysedoucet

Global View

by **Kirsty Hughes**

43(1): 86/87 | DOI: 10.1177/0306422014525113

WITH ELECTIONS COMING up in three of the big G20 democracies in the next few months – India, Indonesia and Brazil – will the tussle for power mean the neglect of free speech and other human rights? Or will new governments, and more debate, mean a chance for progress?

These questions are more important than ever, now that the credibility of the US and UK as defenders of freedom of expression has been undermined by the revelations of mass surveillance of electronic communications around the world by the US National Security Agency (NSA) and the UK Government Communications Headquarters. Democratic countries are in the majority in the G20 – but it's vital they all stand up for free speech in a tougher and more consistent manner.

President Dilma Rousseff has made a strong stand against the impact and implications of the NSA's intrusive surveillance on countries around the world including Brazil

In these three big and increasingly influential democracies, there are both positive and negative signs. India's general election comes first in May, with Indonesia's presidential election due in July, and Brazil facing presidential and congressional elections in early October. Robust and vibrant debates and campaigns can be expected.

But corruption remains a big problem. All three countries are at middle levels in Transparency International's annual corruption perceptions index – with India and Indonesia at a level of 36 and 32 (where 100 counts as transparent and 1 as not transparent) and Brazil a bit ahead at 42.

Corruption undermines democratic processes and can also drive censorship. Demands to remove politically sensitive remarks and criticism from the internet are a serious problem in all three countries, particularly in India and Indonesia. In Brazil, Google's top executive in the country was arrested in 2012 for refusing to take down a YouTube video that included criticism of a local candidate at a mayoral election.

At the same time, social media use is proliferating in all three countries, and as smartphone prices fall and access widens, internet usage is on a sharply upward trend. In India, the main political parties all have social media communication strategies for their election campaigns for the first time. Some hope that this will encourage a more open attitude to social media by India's political elites, whoever wins the election. Others see this as wishful thinking.

Certainly, India's laws (similar to equally negative UK ones) that criminalise "grossly harmful" or "harassing" language on social media and make internet service providers remove content within 36 hours of complaints, must change. But attempts to amend internet technology rules have stalled in India's Senate.

Sensitivity to religious offence and criticism also often drive censorship and attacks on free speech in India and Indonesia, and to a lesser extent in Brazil, with religious minorities in Indonesia facing major human rights abuses, including suppression of free expression.

All three countries have the opportunity to make a major contribution to international digital freedom debates. Brazil is particularly interesting here, and President Dilma Rousseff has made a strong stand against the impact and implications of the NSA's intrusive surveillance on countries around the world including Brazil. And, with the Marco Civil bill, Brazil has developed – but is yet to pass – some of the most progressive digital legislation yet.

But there are risks too. Rousseff has called for legislation to force local hosting of local content by the big internet giants. This is perhaps understandable in response to the NSA revelations – but it would also drive fragmentation of the internet, and be only too welcome as a model for control in countries such as Iran and China.

Elections in these three major democracies present a moment where free speech – for politicians, citizens and the media – is vital and often inspiring. The challenge, not only in the elections, but afterwards, is for these democracies to show they will defend and promote free speech at home and internationally once in power. ☒

Kirsty Hughes is CEO of Index on Censorship

ABOVE: Budapest at night

Credit: Art Kowalsky/Alamy

In this section

Insider state

43(1): 88/95 | DOI: 10.1177/0306422014522574

Hungary's right-wing government has become the pariah of Europe because of its nationalist rhetoric. Ahead of the election **Irena Maryniak** listens to the chorus of voices defending the shift and reports on what liberal critics are calling a "mafia state"

→ **INSIDE PEST'S GRAND** and crumbling apartment blocks the heat is flavoured with a hint of gas, but energy providers take scant interest in minor leaks. People open windows, smile apologetically and prepare to field my routine questions on the state of the nation.

Is Hungary a rising neo-fascist state? "*You mustn't misunderstand. It's a form of populism...*"

And the racism? The intolerance? "*There's a growing gypsy population. In some villages they haven't worked for generations. We have Roma crime. It's a self-perpetuating situation. There's no real anti-semitism, you know.*"

What about the new memorial to Miklos Horthy, a pro-Nazi leader who oversaw the Hungarian Holocaust? "*Pure provocation from extremists. But his contribution needs to be objectively reassessed. Remember the Treaty of Trianon. They dismembered us in 1920. Before that we were occupied by the Turks, the Austrians, the Soviets... Surely you understand?*"

And those vigilantes with licence to rough up and intimidate? "*You mean 'keepers of the peace' – just a traditional gendarmerie. Though there are others...*"

Authoritarianism? Autocracy? Totalitarianism? "*Oh for Chrissake, wasn't it ever thus? Look, you won't quote me will you? It could be awkward. I might get letters. Let me show you out – the doors are a bit heavy. There's a barred archway beyond the inner courtyard. I'll get the electronic key.*"

Hungary is engaged in a cold war over its own story. As the 2014 parliamentary election approaches, the struggle is for the legitimation of narratives – cultural and social, tolerable and intolerable – in a society that has lost its ambling, mellow disposition and seems perilously on edge.

The formerly centre-right governing party, Fidesz – which has long since abandoned any vestige of centrism – holds a two-thirds majority in parliament and has a storyline that dominates Hungarian politics, couched in a combination of nationalist and radical rhetoric. Voters are wooed with emotive catchphrases conjuring images of an ordered, value-based society adrift in a waning Europe infested with exploitative capitalist monopolies.

But at the helm, setting the country firmly on course, is a straight-talking freedom fighter: Prime Minister Viktor Orban. On the eve of his landslide victory in 2010, he spoke of "a revolution in the ballot box". A declaration issued shortly afterwards referred to "a new social contract for the country", a "shared new system of national cooperation" representing "a requirement for every Hungarian at home and abroad". In January 2012, a new constitution was brought into force for a national community bound by "intellectual and spiritual" fabric.

The notion of an ethnically and culturally defined society pervades the education system: previously suppressed writers with far-right connections, including Joszef Nyiro and and Albert Wass, who both had links with the fascist regime of the 1940s, have been introduced into the school curriculum. It is reflected in widespread displays of the national flag (currently flying on parliament alongside the banner of a Hungarian minority in Romania); in the image of that archetypal family gathered around a pot of steaming stew; in the increasing emphasis on the role of women as home-makers and mothers. The government has devoted massive resources to its communications machine.

It is hard to be sure how far the call to close ranks is intended as a boost to flagging spirits in a country of just 10 million, and how far it may be serving a more sinister purpose. The economic crisis left Hungary badly hit. The government has no room for manoeuvre in terms of austerity measures; unemployment among the young is at 28 per cent (10 per cent overall). The fact that many of the jobless are ethnically Roma only adds to a suppressed anxiety and tension.

Fidesz's bid to unite and strengthen Hungarian culture in the Carpathian basin might attract greater external sympathy if its legislative action and approach to the economy was more inclusive and less blatantly partisan. The government has established itself as the strongest voice in public media and reinforced its position through the financial and administrative control of institutional frameworks and of the arts. A new constitution, known as the Fundamental Law, adopted in 2012, seems designed to distance, muffle or suppress voices and groups that might impede the entrenchment of a crony-based "soft" dictatorship: minorities, the poor, the homeless, artists and intellectuals, the media, the judiciary and the constitutional court.

The outraged response of the EU to constitutional amendments introduced in March 2013 is well documented. The changes seemed a flagrant assault on democratic rights and liberties. In June, the Council of Europe noted "the sheer accumulation of reforms that aim to establish political control of most key institutions while in parallel weakening the system of checks and balances". Rather than open a monitoring procedure, however, it chose "closely to follow the situation in Hungary and take stock of the progress achieved".

Critics say the fundamental law was adopted without serious debate, following a "national consultation" that consisted of 12 multiple-choice questions posted with a barcode that made identification possible. Given that, in 2010, Fidesz party director Gabor Kubatov suggested the existence of an online database with voters' details ("I can point to the Communists in the city," he said), a comment that was leaked to the public on the right-wing portal kuruc.info and in the English language newspaper Budapest Times, many felt there was good reason to be troubled.

"Those who do not support Fidesz have the perception that, although the elections are supposed to be free and fair and secret, ultimately some people have these databases and they know who is voting for whom," Petra Bard, visiting professor at the Central European University, observes.

ABOVE: Members of the far-right Hungarian Guard stand next to the unveiled bust of Miklos Horthy, Hungary's World War II ruler, Csokako, Hungary, 2012. The erection of the statue met with criticism from the country's liberal contingent

Credit: Bela Szandelszky/AP/PA

This spring, a majority of a little over 50 per cent would give Fidesz absolute supremacy

Previously suppressed writers with far-right connections have been introduced into the school curriculum

in parliament. Few doubt that it will get it. Hungarians living outside the country have been offered citizenship and the vote. A traditionally conservative group, they are →

→ expected to rally behind the government. Last year energy bills were cut by 20 per cent – which has raised support further. All this, combined with alleged gerrymandering in some districts and an election law that favours large parties over small, is likely to benefit Fidesz. To make a protest vote count, people will have to opt for the Socialist Party (MSzP), which has its origins in the pre-1989 (Communist) Socialist Workers Party (MSzMP). With memories still fresh of eight years of disappointing rule by a socialist-liberal coalition (2002-10), voters will almost certainly shy away from this. The MSzP is still hampered by its association with communism and is further disadvantaged by the absence of allies on the left.

The openly anti-Roma party Jobbik, in parliament since 2010, has the support of about 15 per cent of the electorate

In response to European pressure, the government grudgingly introduced a few corrective measures to the constitution. The media have been given the right to broadcast political advertising – provided they do so for free. Observers are doubtful that economically hard-pressed commercial television channels will be in any position to screen meaningful political debate. News stories are centralised and controlled through the Hungarian News Agency (MTI) and, since 2010, broadcasts have been regulated by the National Media and Infocommunications Authority (NMHH), whose president holds a mandate for nine years. The NMHH also controls the budget, and its jurisdiction covers broadcast, print and online public and private media including blogs. It has the power to assign frequencies, monitor content and impose fines. In 2011, penalties for media providers came to 1.4 million euros. "There are more and more cases where the court fines in favour of politicians who are applicants and who allegedly have been defamed," says Petra Bard. Since new media laws came into force, more than 500 journalists from public broadcasters have lost their jobs.

Journalists refer to an all pervasive culture of political loyalty. A liberal former minister of education, Balint Magyar, talks of blackmail and threats to commercial media, alongside the enforced nationalisation and subsequent privatisation of business in favour of friends and cronies. "You can see it in the field of public utilities, in the bank sector, the land sector, effectively everywhere," he says.

Loyalty can be coerced and dissent punished through tax inspection, for example. Businesses are intimidated or rewarded with government contracts and licences – whether for tobacco sales, or broadcasting. Most commercial channels prefer to stay out of politics. The threat of lost state-dependent advertising – by the national oil company MOL or the OTP banking group, for example) – serves as a lever for controlling the private broadcasting sector. "There's no need for direct political pressure or Soviet-style telephone rule," says a journalist (who asks not to be named). "You know what you can and can't do. It's the same system as in the 1970s and 80s. There's an ingrained cultural sensitivity."

In some circles there is talk of disgruntled opposition figures outside the country stirring up western European suspicion and giving Hungary a bad name. In January 2012, a group of internationally known liberal intellectuals, including Miklos Haraszti, the former MP and UN Special Rapporteur on Belarus, and Gyorgy Konrad, the writer, published an appeal which referred to the end of genuine debate and accountable governance in Hungary, calling on Europe to help prevent a slide into dictatorship: "Victor Orban's government is intent on destroying the democratic rule of law, removing checks and balances and pursuing a systematic policy of closing all autonomous institutions...At no point since the regime changes of 1989...has there been such an intense concentration of power in the region as in present-day Hungary."

The push by liberals to draw the rest of Europe into the Hungarian political picture is viewed with intense suspicion among government sympathisers. In a deeply polarised political community, liberal views are widely perceived to be associated with the Alliance of Free Democrats (SzDSz) a party in coalition with the socialists between 1994 and 2008. "It's hard to take their criticism as an honest critique," says Mark Szabo, an analyst at the right-wing think tank, the Central European Policy Centre. "It's misleading to portray their views as the views of independent intellectuals. They are people institutionally identified with SzDSz. They have a bias – which is natural. What is not acceptable is that they criticise as though they were neutral players in the game, which they are not."

Today the SzDSz barely exists as a political force – in 2010 the party won just 0.25 per cent of the vote – but the voices of its former representatives and sympathisers count. These are the people who present an ideological challenge to Fidesz.

"The problem is that Fidesz has its own language through which it creates its narratives. Until now the opposition has been in an exclusively defensive position," says Balint Magyar. "It had no language to describe the real nature of the regime. If you cannot describe or name what you oppose you are bound to be defeated. You have to decide: are you fighting within the structure of liberal democracy for government change or does Hungary have a new form of regime which is neither 'liberal' nor 'majority' democracy but something quite different – a mafia state."

"Mafia" is a hackneyed word in the eastern European context, but it offers a framework to challenge the Fidesz narrative. The idea is developed in a selection of essays by liberal academics, some of them former politicians, published in a book edited by Balint Magyar, Hungarian Octopus: The Post-Communist Mafia State. The book has been reprinted three times since its publication in November 2013. The model is familiar in many post-Soviet republics, including Russia. What the traditional mafia achieve by threat and murder, Magyar contends, the "mafia state" state can achieve through parliament, the tax office, the chief attorney, and all the organs of the state. "They distort the conditions of free elections, of freedom of speech, the neutrality of state organs, public procurement procedures. There is brainwashing and money laundering, power concentration and concentration of personal wealth.

"There is brainwashing and money laundering, power concentration and concentration of personal wealth"

Western Europe has to face the fact that tax payers are subsidising the Hungarian mafia state, and its adopted 'family'. Traditional categories of 'corruption' cannot explain or describe the situation and western European countries have no effective means to sanction it. Hungary is a Trojan Horse in the EU."

Magyar advocates greater international involvement in decision-making, and in committees for the evaluation of EU tenders, but among the Hungarian population the issue of outside involvement in Hungary's affairs is highly sensitive. People often fear "the outside": centuries of occupation are not that easily forgotten. To the horrified delight of many, Prime Minister Viktor Orban has appeared to draw parallels between the EU and the Soviet Union.

A 40-something lawyer, who asks not to be named, speaks of a sense of shame associated with Hungarian identity, which only Fidesz has successfully dispelled. "If I →

→ had Hungarian thoughts – about the loss of Transylvania for example – I used to be called irredentist or racist. Now I can have my own thoughts. Our generation was taught we were a loser nation. We were all but criminals. We had a right to be punished. It was a communist trick. They tried to make people feel guilty. Fidesz was the first to say this. Now people can be proud of their history and their achievements, proud to be here."

There is a flip side to this. Earlier failures to objectively examine issues associated with national self-perception and historical trauma – the Horthy era between 1920 and 1944 or the "goulash communism" of Janos Kadar – have licensed the exploitation of historical memory. The differentiation between an unsullied and rational "self", and a morally soiled, exploitative or barbaric "other" is as much a part of Hungarian political culture as ever it was. In January 2013,

Orban himself thrives on his bold challenges to foreigners and European bureaucrats

Zsolt Bayer, a co-founder of Fidesz, wrote in response to a stabbing of two youths – allegedly by Gypsy assailants – that Roma were "animals...incapable of human communication" and "should not be allowed to exist".

The openly anti-Roma party Jobbik, in parliament since 2010, has the support of about 15 per cent of the electorate. The party has spruced up its image recently, offering itself as a cool, hard-talking alternative to Fidesz. It is increasingly popular among young voters. People at the centre of the political spectrum express anxiety, because there have been surprises – not least the election on 15 December of a notorious neo-Nazi as mayor of Asotthalom, a village close to the Serbian border. Laszlo Toroczkai took 71 per cent of the vote in a contest with a Fidesz candidate. Some years ago he declared he would be prepared to shoot former socialist prime minister Ferenc Gyurcsany.

With Jobbik representing a real political threat, Fidesz also plays to the far-right gallery, while distancing itself from some of the more extreme manifestations of fascism (such as the public burning of poetry books by the Holocaust victim Miklos Radnoti in the north-eastern city of Miskolc last November). Orban himself thrives on his bold challenges to foreigners and European bureaucrats, and his supporters suggest European officials critical of Hungary are generating the very anti-European sentiment that could empower anti-EU forces and the far right.

How is the public responding to all this? "Most Hungarians simply want a strong leader," says one journalist. "They don't want the difficulties of capitalism, having to decide their own personal and financial future."

Fidesz has learnt from the past; the left is tarnished by it. Attempts to form an opposition alliance, called Together 2014, have reaped few dividends, not least because of an absence of persuasive or charismatic leadership. But, despite the government's efforts to constrain the outreach of independent media, it would be misleading to suggest that its opponents have been wholly silenced. The private channel ATV is the main television platform for broader discussion on politics, along with the news and talk radio station Klub Radio – which was threatened with closure in September 2011 but survived after an international outcry and a series of court battles. There are several independent press outlets: newspapers Nepszabadsag, Nepszava, and the economic weekly HVG. NGOs take some comfort in coverage by internet-based news portals. The most popular of these, Index.hu, has 1.3 million readers monthly.

Any hope for Hungarian democracy and politics almost certainly lies with online media and a new generation of activists. In 2013, students throughout the country protested against cuts in funded university places, increases in tuition fees and the introduction of a contract obliging them to work in Hungary after graduating. Demonstrations against the media law and electoral legislation favouring Fidesz, in 2011, were followed by protests against the new Fundamental Law the following year. Tens of thousands participated in the rallies. Rapper Dorottya Karsay's soundtrack of the protest movement, "*Nem tetszik a rendszer*", has clocked up over 1.3 million hits on YouTube.

The title and the refrain could scarcely be clearer: "I don't, I don't, I don't like the system." ☒

Irena Maryniak is a regular contributor to Index on Censorship and the magazine's former eastern European editor

Poland and the new anti-semitism

43(1): 96/99 | DOI: 10.1177/0306422013520285

With the experience of Communist censorship still fresh in many peoples' minds, Polish people have resisted government attempts to control free speech. But, argues journalist **Konstanty Gebert**, this has meant local prosecutors are reluctant to stamp out anti-semitism, even when the foreign minister is a target

"THIS WAS SUPPOSED to be a democracy, and yet everybody says what they think!" This apocryphal quote, attributed to former Polish president Lech Wałesa, not only neatly exemplifies the leader's idiosyncratic rhetoric, but also points to democracy's freedom of speech paradox.

While freedom of expression is the foundation of any democracy, it is also true that things people say can actually pose a mortal threat to democracy. While many might agree that such speech should be restricted, there is not, and probably cannot be, any agreement as to where to draw the line.

Poland, a successful democracy for almost a quarter of a century now, is extremely reluctant to penalise any kind of free expression. By being so markedly liberal, however, the country is supporting illiberal ideologies, which often derive more profit from the right to free speech than ideologies that might be defined as liberal or progressive.

In June 2013, Wojciech Zaleski, head of a regional prosecutor's office for the north-eastern city of Białystok-North, refused to prosecute people who painted swastikas on the walls of several buildings in the city because, as he explained, "The swastika is an Asian symbol of good fortune" and so can be legally displayed. Over the last few years, Białystok has become a hotbed of extremist violence. There have been instances of refugees being attacked on the street and apartments belonging to couples of different ethnic backgrounds being set on fire. Shoah memorials have been vandalised and racist graffiti daubed on walls. The police have been unable to identify the perpetrators, and a government-led investigation indicated that the government itself had in some cases been infiltrated by extreme right-wing militants.

Zaleski's opinion seemed to fit nicely with the mood, but it proved nonetheless to be too much. In September, after the general public expressed outrage over his comments, Zaleski resigned from his post to avoid being fired. It goes without saying that the author of the "good fortune" graffiti has never been identified.

The instinct for leniency shown by the prosecutor is perhaps not surprising given that the experience of Communist censorship is fresh in many peoples' minds, and Poland generally still remains allergic to the idea that the government should decide what can and cannot be said.

And yet it seems that leniency is proffered most often to those who hurl anti-semitic insults. In June 2013, another prosecutor, this time in the city of Kielce in central Poland, refused to classify the public use of the term "Jewish carcass" as an insult. The prosecutor's office later reconsidered, possibly because of the city's history. In 1946, 42 Jews were murdered in Kielce in Europe's largest post-World War II pogrom, so a certain sensitivity to the term "Jewish carcasses" might understandably linger there.

When reaching his decision, the Kielce prosecutor did not use the argument that the term is insulting only if directed at an actual Jew. That honour was given to the prosecutor's office in Lublin, in the southeast of the country. In 2012, the prosecutor decided not to investigate a case where a professor at the local university used the words "dirty Jewess" when arguing with another professor about the use of a seminar room.

The Lublin prosecutor was of the opinion that as the professor targeted was "Polish, not Jewish", even though she taught Jewish studies, it was impossible for her to regard this comment as an insult.

But the chairman of the Union of Jewish Religious Communities, Piotr Kadlčik, was worried enough by this and similar events to write a letter to the prosecutor general and to the minister of the interior, which led to the two officials meeting to coordinate their efforts against anti-semitism. The chairman had a legitimate right to feel concern: of the 473 race crimes reported in 2012, fewer than half were investigated. The largest number of attacks, 98, targeted Jews; followed by attacks against those defined as black, Roma, Arab and Muslim. It is important to stress that most crimes are not reported, because victims, not without reason, believe racist attacks will not be investigated.

Even so, anti-semitism manifests itself much less overtly and publicly today than it did 15 years ago. Gone are the days when anti-semitic publications could be bought on newsstands; when the notorious anti-semitic text favoured by the Nazis, The Protocols of the Elders of Zion, was prominently displayed in some churches; or when the walls of some Polish houses were adorned with pictures of the Star of David hanging from gallows.

In September 2013, Professor Ireneusz Krzeminski of the Polish Academy of Sciences published the results of a survey of

Over the last few years, Białystok has become a hotbed of extremist violence. There have been instances of refugees being attacked on the street and apartments belonging to couples of different ethnic backgrounds being set on fire

anti-semitism in Poland. It found that in 2012, 20 per cent of Poles expressed "modern" anti-semitism, which was defined as a negative view of the role of Jews in public life. The report also said that 8 per cent of the population displayed "traditional" anti-semitism, referring to the belief that Jews' theological position was wrong. According to data published in 2002, 27 per cent of the population subscribed to "modern" anti-semitism and 11.6 per cent to "traditional". For 1992, the figures were 17 per cent and 11.5 per cent respectively.

This decline of anti-semitism is due in part to shifting opinions among Poles, as well as an understanding that in the →

ABOVE: Defaced graves, Jewish cemetery, Czestochowa

→ country that had experienced the Shoah first-hand, manifestations of anti-semitism are particularly damning. But these overt forms of anti-semitism are also on the decrease because of a certain amount of repression, however inadequate.The targets of hatred are changing too.

Across Poland, homophobic and misogynic attitudes are expressed on a wide scale. According to the European Union Agency

The fact that virulent anti-semitic opinions are freely expressed by Polish trolls presents any liberal with a problem

for Fundamental Rights' 2013 report on homophobia in Europe, 63 per cent of the Polish lesbian, gay, bisexual, and transgender community reported that discrimination on the grounds of sexual orientation was widespread, though it was worse in Lithuania, Croatia and Romania. And yet successfully prosecuting homophobic acts is no less difficult than prosecuting other hate crimes.

There are occasional prosecutions, for instance for "insult to religious feelings", a crime punishable under Polish law by a fine or up to two years' imprisonment. These prosecutions, if rare, are always widely commented on in the Polish press, as those insulted are almost always Catholics, Poland's majority religion. Recently, Karol Szwalbe, a newly-appointed police chief in the town of Radom, was denounced for this crime after removing a cross from the wall of his office, which had been put there by a predecessor. The local prosecutor has not yet said whether he will take up the case.

After being convicted on charges of insulting religion for saying the Bible had been written "by a guy high on wine and grass", pop singer Dorota Rabczewska lodged an appeal with the Supreme Court. She was the only person convicted of the crime in 2012. There were no convictions in 2011, six in 2010 and 13 in 2009.

Had Rabczewska made her comments online rather than in an interview, she would have probably not been charged. In general, prosecutors have avoided responding to online material; the "Jewish carcass" case in Kielce was a rare exception. On the whole, the internet is left unregulated, as Polish foreign minister Radek Sikorski, who is married to the Washington Post columnist Anne Applebaum, discovered. Repeatedly denounced by anti-semitic bloggers and trolls as a "Jew" and "Jewish agent" because of his liberal policies and because of his wife, who is of Jewish heritage, he tried to persuade the prosecutor's office to investigate the abuse as a hate crime. He hit a brick wall.

The office's opinion was that Sikorski could lodge a lawsuit himself if he felt offended, but that the office would not intervene, especially as he himself is not Jewish (and therefore, according to the interpretation applied in the case of the academic, cannot be slandered). It was also made clear that the chances of identifying those responsible for the comments were slim. Sikorski declined to file a lawsuit, believing that such speech harms not only his own interests, but

Credit: Peter Andrews/Reuters

those of the state, and should be prosecuted ex officio. If a government minister cannot persuade prosecutors to take action, what are the chances of others having success?

The Polish-language internet is overflowing with hate speech, especially of the anti-semitic variety. This applies to comments on news items or op-eds addressing contemporary Jewish life, or regarding Israel. Some leading internet portals have blocked discussions relating to these topics because of the prolific anti-semitism they provoke. But even less obvious subjects trigger an anti-semitic response. In August 2012 the Polish news site wp.pl published a short news story about the appointment of Dan Sova, a Holocaust denier, as minister for parliamentary relations in Romania, and the protests by Jewish organisations that ensued. The post immediately attracted attention: 367 people commented on the site, while, in Romania, these sorts of news items would generate, on average, around six comments per news item.

Of the comments posted, 12.5 per cent responded directly to what Sova had said regarding the Holocaust, expressing support for his views or attacking his critics. Slightly more, 13.8 per cent, were more general comments unrelated to Sova's views. But the overwhelming majority of comments, 70.2 per cent, expressed outrage at Jews, either for spreading "the lie of the Shoah", or for other "crimes". The remaining comments, 4.5 per cent, or 12 posts, expressed either sympathy for Jewish people or horror about Holocaust denial. These figures suggest a worrying trend and an unequivocal truth about the level of anti-semitism among a significant number of Polish internet trolls. Many people also responded positively to rhetorical questions like, "What about European Jews who deny the Israeli occupation? What about the crimes of Israel and the suffering of Palestinians?" But in this case, although this type of denial does exist in Poland, the specific wording is not considered to be anti-semitic, regardless of intent. Other statements are more directly anti-semitic. Typical is the accusation that while Jews had undoubtedly suffered in the World War II, non-Jewish Poles suffered no less, and then suffered again at Jewish hands under Communism – meanwhile Jews turned their suffering into a shameful business. Such statements are met with virtually no criticism. After all, it requires no great effort to click the "thumb down" icon next to a comment, and this is as significant as the unambiguous, overt anti-semitic statements themselves. The fact that virulent anti-semitic opinions are freely expressed by Polish trolls presents any liberal with a problem. On the one hand, engaging in a discussion with somebody who believes that a new Shoah would be desirable is plainly impossible. Even if one were to do so, however, one would then support this opinion as a legitimate expression. Yet refusing to engage might suggest there is no counter-argument.

Prosecution would send the clear signal that such opinions are not acceptable. Even if chances of identifying the author are slim, and even if the entire question of limits of free speech were to be re-opened again, this seems to be preferable to resigning oneself to inaction. ☒

Konstanty Gebert is a regular contributor to Gazeta Wyborcza and the founder of Jewish magazine Midrasz. He was a leading Solidarity journalist and co-founder of the Jewish Flying University in 1979 and the Polish Council of Christians and Jews in 1989

Stories of the shutdown

43(1): 101/105 | DOI: 10.1177/0306422014521342

Thousands of scientists across the US feel cutbacks are seriously restricting their research and contributions. **Gretchen Goldman** asks scientists for their reaction and about impact on their work

SCIENTISTS IN THE United States have experienced their fair share of censorship. Last year's partial shutdown of government has left the federal scientific community facing an even more uncertain future.

The crisis began in March 2013, when the US government's budget was sequestered, leading to immediate automatic cuts in public spending. Then in October, amid further political wrangles about the budget, the government closed down for two and a half weeks. Both events had serious implications for the rights to free speech of scientists working for or with the federal government.

With ongoing budget concerns and no prospects for revived public science funding on the horizon, the possibility of long-term detrimental consequences for federal science in the US looms large.

Actions taken during the George W Bush administration made it considerably more difficult for scientists to share publicly their research, and while there has been some improvement on that front, a whole new set of systemic challenges now undermines these scientists' right to free speech. Nearly every federal science agency and programme saw their budget slashed by five per cent. Many programmes were no longer sustainable. There was a drastic decrease in the number and size of federal grants awarded to scientists both inside and outside government. Some laboratories were forced to close, and some researchers lost their jobs.

Scientists who survived the cuts were forced to work with newly imposed restrictions. Federal scientists were essentially barred from attending conferences; the unanticipated budget cuts led many federal agencies to make policy changes, resctricting how many scientists could attend a given conference. Or they implemented no-travel policies altogether. In fact even scientists scheduled to deliver keynote speeches at prestigious events, including ones that had been planned for months or even years, were forced to cancel their appearances at short notice.

The right to attend conferences is part of scientific free speech. Conferences are where ideas are fostered and collaborations born. Scientific free speech includes the right of scientists to express their professional and personal opinions on a topic, and this also includes the right to publish and contribute meaningfully to the scientific community. In other words, scientific free speech is the right to be a scientist.

Most scientists tolerated this restriction. After all, it was thought to be a temporary →

→ impediment. As it turned out, the effects of the sequestration were only the tip of the iceberg.

On 1 October 2013, the US government went into a partial shutdown because of Congress' failure to approve a budget for the fiscal year 2014. During the 16-day shutdown - the third longest in US history - the government sent hundreds of thousands of federal workers and contractors on temporary leave and many programmes and services were suspended. Again, the scientific community's right to free speech was undermined, this time with even more of an impact than had been felt under the sequester.

Eleven days into the shutdown, the Union of Concerned Scientists sent email enquiries to 20,000 Science Network members about the impact of the federal government shutdown on their ability to do their work. The network comprises scientists and other technical experts from across the US. They span a wide range of scientific fields, ages, employers and geographic locations. Some are employed by the federal government, and many more receive federal funding, use government facilities, or rely on federally produced data or other resources to carry out their work.

The shutdown was largely a huge, unplanned experiment in what happens when we give up on science for two weeks

Within hours, the union received a wide range of stories, testifying to the breadth of impacts being felt across the scientific community, from graduate students to principle investigators, from public health officials to field biologists. The following are some of the comments and sentiments expressed in the survey responses:

Firstly, at a fundamental level, the shutdown closed off basic communication within the scientific community. Many government scientists were not allowed to access email, much less their laboratories. One scientist noted that his "direct supervisor ... confiscated all laptop computers on the day of the shutdown".

Without access to work email accounts, federal scientists were also prevented from carrying out professional activities that went beyond their government job duties. Several scientists pointed out that their inability to access emails significantly slowed down the peer-review process and, therefore, journal publication.

These restrictions on communication were not limited to federal employees. During the shutdown, many scientists did not have access to government databases or government lands. One scientist explained: "Almost all of the NASA data sites that I use for my research have been shut down. This seriously impacts my analyses." Another scientist working for a small non-profit company relies completely on government supercomputers because the organisation does not have the computer power to run their own computer models.

The shutdown had a detrimental impact on students and early career scientists in particular. One PhD student explained that the majority of her dissertation research is performed on a US Fish and Wildlife Service refuge and though she did not need the help of federal employees to conduct her work, she was locked out of the land during the shutdown. One early-career researcher had a "once-in-a-lifetime opportunity to travel to Antarctica" to do field work on long-term climate variations. After the trip was cancelled, she lamented the "millions of dollars that will have been squandered" and noted the "ripple effect" for future researchers.

This kind of disruption, even if brief, can have serious consequences for graduate students and early career scientists, who often rely on narrow time windows to conduct their research. Environmentally sensitive

ABOVE: The US Capitol behind a chain link fence, 30 September 2013, on the eve of the two-week government closure

Credit: Kevin Lamarque/Reuters

field studies, time-limited funding, and other factors mean graduate students and young scientists are often working on tight deadlines. Missed opportunities for research can have serious setbacks, as they may delay how quickly scientists can publish, obtain tenure in academic positions and build a solid footing on which to build their career in competitive scientific fields.

One scientist shared the impact the shutdown had on a research group at the Environmental Protection Agency charged with addressing water quality issues on indigenous reservations. Again, travel restrictions were a chief concern. "An emergency site visit to a tribal water system in New Mexico with bacterial contamination in their well was cancelled," the scientist said. The meeting would have included the state Environmental Protection Agency, tribal officials and the parent water system that was involved in the sale of contaminated water.

According to the chair of an internal science panel related to water resources and climate, participation by US federal scientists in meetings that had been planned for over a year was withdrawn for two October meetings. The meetings went ahead as planned, but "without involvement of US scientific leaders". One scientist commented →

→ that this outcome has been "downright embarrassing for scientists in the US". In another example, the National Climate Assessment, a consensus document produced every few years by the nation's leading climate experts, was brought to a standstill as all coordination between government scientists and outside experts was halted.

Long-term impacts

Following the restrictions on scientists and the undermining of federal science under the George W Bush administration, the Union of Concerned Scientists, demoralised federal scientists and their supporters came together to advocate for changes in policy to ensure federal scientists enjoyed full free speech rights and were less vulnerable to political interference. Many improvements were implemented, including scientific integrity policies from 22 federal agencies. These included the right to express personal views, the right to publish, and enhanced whistleblower protections. The progress made, however, may in future be limited if inadequate resources prevent federal scientists from doing their work.

A second round of cuts in 2014 is a very real possibility

There are huge ramifications for scientists' freedom to conduct their work. Many of the shutdown's impacts on scientists may be permanent. This is especially true for scientists in time-limited programmes and funding sources, for example, research conducted by the National Institute of Health. Scientists from all disciplines need an open environment with reliable, dependable funding so that they can help deliver crucial public services.

"In the long term, the US lead in scientific research and technology will suffer," said one senior scientist who uses government data for his work, basing his predictions on the morale of colleagues. This fear was echoed by early career scientists, some of whom considered seeking alternative work unconnected with government agencies. In some cases, these scientists considered looking for work outside of the country altogether.

A research entomologist with the US Department of Agriculture commented, "It seems time to consider other ways of paying my salary if the government puts so little value on science." Another worried about the challenges of securing future funding from government sources, explaining that "moving to a country like the UK or other parts of Europe, which have much more stable funding structure[s] and overall support for scientists, may be a better career choice." An astrophysicist who works closely with researchers at the National Aeronautics and Space Administration (NASA) keenly observed, "I am seeing a long term effect on my colleagues' attitudes about their scientific research. Even senior researchers feel that their work is not valued. Funding has been cut severely even before the shutdown. Younger scientists have become disillusioned."

As Andrew Rosenberg, director of the Center for Science and Democracy at the Union of Concerned Scientists, has put it, the shutdown was largely "a huge, unplanned experiment in what happens when we give up on science for two weeks."

If the shutdown had been an isolated incident in an otherwise thriving scientific enterprise, its effects on scientists might have been minimal. Some research projects would have been disrupted, creating data gaps in long-term monitoring projects, but scientists would have recovered and research would have continued. The reality, however, is different. Adding the government shutdown to an already deflated group of scientists was a hard blow. Scientific research, already under strain from sequester cuts, now faces bigger challenges and scientists face more restrictions.

The greatest fear is of potential deeper cuts in the near future. The US Congress continues to debate solutions to the federal deficit and a second round of cuts caused by sequestration in 2014 is a very real possibility. The impacts of the 2013 sequester and the subsequent government shutdown were significant, but in some ways federal agencies were able to be resourceful – scraping up funds from less essential reserves and re-allocating current funding to minimise impacts. This year any reserves federal agencies have will be exhausted and they will have less flexibility in their spending. For some federal science programmes, a second round of cuts could be the straw that breaks the camel's back.

Government agencies employ, and government grants fund, some of the top scientific minds in the US. But the progress of science depends on consistent, reliable institutions to support and stay with projects over long periods of time. To succeed in their work, scientists need the opportunity to exercise their right to scientific free speech. A scientific enterprise that is subject to the volatility of Congressional votes and political sentiment cannot provide this. It's essential for the government to provide the tools and the culture necessary for its scientists and science to thrive.

Gretchen T Goldman is an analyst for the Center for Science and Democracy at the Union of Concerned Scientists

ABOVE: A protester uses her mobile device as she walks at Gezi Park on Taksim Square in Istanbul 6 June 2013. The government has made clear its disapproval of social media services, which are being used more and more as newspapers and television come increasingly under the sway of the state

Credit: Stoyan Nenov/Reuters

Turkey's Twitter army

43(1): 106/110 | DOI: 10.1177/0306422014522385

In Turkey the government has brought together a massive team of social media specialists for the upcoming elections in 2014. But there are already signs of foul-play argues **Kaya Genç**

ONE DAY IN June last year, a Turkish journalist working at the BBC World Service was surprised to find her name on the top of "trending topics", a list generated by the users of the social media website Twitter. In order to make their conversations more focused, Twitter users mark their tweets using hashtags; the hashtag that brought the Turkish journalist to the top of the trending topic list was written in an extremely accusatory tone. It read: *#ingiltereadinaajanlikyapmaselingirit*, which roughly means "Don't spy on behalf of England, Selin Girit."

Selin Girit, based in London since 2007, was a familiar face for Turkish viewers who watched her BBC reports every afternoon on national television until a few weeks after this event (when the Turkish network NTV refused to broadcast a BBC report critical of Turkish media's coverage of protests and the BBC cancelled its contract). →

→ On the day she became a trending topic, Girit was in Turkey to report on the debates inspired by Occupy Wall Street that were taking place in numerous public parks in Istanbul. The violent state response to the environmental protests in Istanbul's Gezi Park had abated but not ended. The Turkish government was doing its best to control the protests on two fronts: on the street and, perhaps more crucially, on social media, where protesters decided on meeting points and discussed new strategies. While listening to a public debate, Girit tweeted what she heard: "Here is a suggestion from the park: let's stop the economy. Let's stop consuming for six months. Then they will have to listen to us."

Melih Gökçek, the mayor of Turkey's capital Ankara, who has more than a million followers on Twitter, was not pleased to see this advice being circulated. Interpreting Girit's tweet as proof of a conspiracy planned in London – hence the accusation of spying for the UK – he started the now infamous hashtag which was used in thousands of tweets. In response to this campaign Twitter users started the hashtag *#selingiritgazetecidir* ("Selin Girit is a journalist") and defended the reporter.

Gökçek's campaign foreshadowed the increasing use of Twitter in political circles in the months that followed. In September there were reports in the media about the governing Justice and Development (AK) Party's 6,000-strong "Twitter Army". Public relations specialists at the party headquarters chose and trained those users, showing them ways to change the conversation on the social media. With the Turkish local elections scheduled for 30 March 2014, the opening shots have been fired in an ideological war in which the social media have the potential to become the main battlefield.

According to a study by the independent market research company eMarketer, Turkey has more than 36 million internet users and 31 per cent use Twitter. This means Turkey has the highest Twitter penetration in the world (followed by Japan, Netherlands and Venezuela). For politicians from all camps, these numbers turn Twitter into an immensely attractive platform for organising election campaigns.

Mustafa Sarıgül, the mayoral candidate for Istanbul and a member of the country's main opposition party, the Republican People's Party (CHP), is among those who have been pouring significant funds into his Twitter campaign. While the Sarıgül Twitter team struggles against AK Party's "Twitter Army" Sarıgül reportedly paid $13,000 dollars per day to Twitter to make his campaign a trending topic every day until the elections. Although these appear as "promoted" or "sponsored" tweets they play an important role in defining the political conversation in the country.

The increased significance of Turkey's social media poses specific challenges in the fields of ethics and freedom of expression. If political parties employ professional Twitter users to inflict the greatest damage to members of the opposing camp, where does that leave us in terms of ethics? Doesn't it take away the free-spirited, individualistic quality of the media and replace it with a digital Machiavellianism where political ends justify digital means? In the polluted atmosphere of Turkish politics this is undoubtedly the case.

According to Ceren Kenar, a columnist in Türkiye newspaper, there is nothing wrong with using Twitter for political means. "Twitter is a venue with its own internal rules," she says. "That a political group wants to be active in this venue is of course legitimate. But the rules that apply to the street do not apply to the digital world: electoral fraud is a crime in the real world whereas a politician can exaggerate his popularity through fake Twitter accounts and get away with it." She points to the lack of a legal framework or code of conduct for such problems. "Twitter was initially a space for self-expression but it suddenly turned into this great apparatus for manipulation or propaganda," she says. According to Kenar, the Turkish Twittersphere echoes and continues some of the unethical practices that have hitherto dominated newspapers and websites, such as serving the interests of political parties by way of inflicting damage on their adversaries without taking journalistic standards into account, and preferring partisanship over proper journalism. This is why the responsibility of producing credible content on Twitter partly falls on the shoulders of journalists who must protect their objectivity even when faced with intimidation. "The only asset a journalist has is reputation," she says. "During the Gezi events some journalists tweeted false information, such as a helicopter throwing bombs at protestors, and there were also conspiracy theorists that connected everything to the Gezi protestors. The media should take a careful look at those journalists who contributed to disinformation."

Twitter also poses challenges in the field of freedom of expression since the volume of digital information its users produce makes the platform very difficult to moderate by Turkish prosecutors. Before Twitter, it was relatively easy for prosecutors to go after websites and successfully shut them down for ideological reasons: YouTube was shut down in its entirety between 2008 and 2010 in Turkey because of a video that allegedly insulted the Turkish political leader Mustafa Kemal. It was only last November that the French video-sharing website Dailymotion was closed for a few weeks. During the Gezi events there were reports of a possible closure of Twitter after the prime minister talked on national television about the social media being "the worst menace to society".

The irony of the Prime Minister's position was that when he expressed it in front of the cameras his advisers were busy formulating those same arguments in 140 character-long tweets. So Turkey's politicians by no means downplay the importance of Twitter. Perhaps the problem is that they take it too seriously.

Just consider the case of Gökçek, the Ankara mayor, who had drawn a parallel between debates on Twitter and battles fought in ancient wars. "As long as we tweet with an intensity similar to that of our love for worship, our enemies do give up," he said in July last year. "By learning how to use Twitter better we will take the ammunition away from them. Foreign power centres start revolutions and coups through the social media... If our grandmothers, grandfathers and *hadjis* learn how to use this thing, then we will triumph."

Gökçek's call for mobilisation on Twitter had its parallel in the anti-government camp, where the influential hacktivist group RedHack had for long been collaborating with a group of devoted protestors to disseminate

Those developments were but the opening shots in an ideological war where the social media has the potential to become the main battlefield

information on public servants and leading government figures. In February and March last year, the group started a full-fledged war against the Ankara municipality and hacked its website. In June they used Twitter to publish mobile numbers of parliamentarians whom they accused of being insensitive about the events in Gezi Park. They also made public the contact information of high-ranking police chiefs whom they denounced for being responsible for the heavy-handed response to protestors. In October 2012, the cyber-crimes branch of Turkish police force had detained 10 RedHack activists whom the public prosecutor accused of providing digital aid to terrorist groups. The group's support for Gezi events made them more suspect in the eyes of the security →

→ community. If convicted, they could face up to 24 years in prison.

In this very politicised atmosphere Twitter seems to have been taken up with enthusiasm among Turkish politicians and journalists. It has become the de facto platform for politicians to express their positions, a space where they make politics around the clock and get instant reaction. This also leads to occasional Twitter feuds between Turkish politicians and journalists. After the liberal Taraf newspaper published documents about the government's data-collecting activities in November, a parliamentarian from the governing party called the journalist who broke the story "a dog". When such heated exchanges take place on Twitter, journalists and politicians sometimes retreat and apologise, but the damage is done for the moment and then the apologies, when they are made, rarely attract the same amount of interest from the public.

Until the elections are over in April we will probably see more examples of intense 140-character-long exchanges and it is a good thing that we can read them without the interference of censorship. Politicians may have called it "the worst menace to society" but none of them dared to censor Twitter or close it down — with so many voters actively using the website it would amount to nothing less than political suicide. ☒

Kaya Genç is a novelist and essayist based in Istanbul, Turkey. He tweets @kayagenc

Credit: Andy Clark/Reuters

ABOVE: Protesters dressed as scientists take part in an Evidence for Democracy demonstration in Vancouver, during September 2013. The group is protesting recent federal government cuts in scientific work and rules regarding releasing of information to the public.

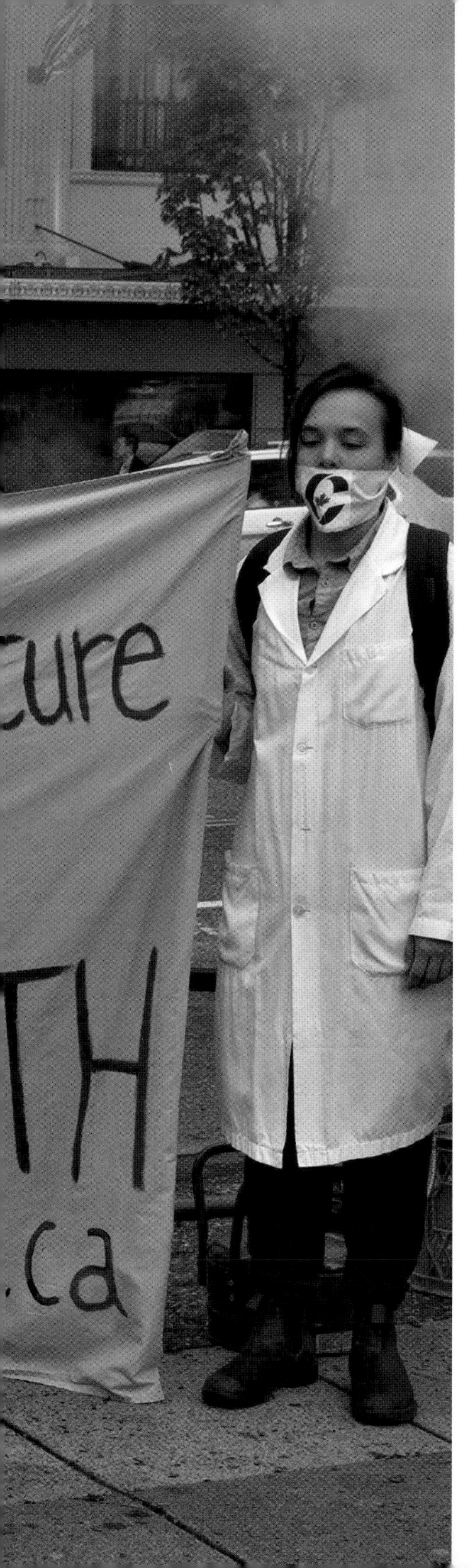

The day the earth moved

43(1): 112/118 | DOI: 10.1177/0306422014521360

Canadian scientists are being prevented by the state from discussing research findings in public, even about earthquakes in their backyard. **Mark Frary** reports

ON WEDNESDAY 24 June 2010, something very unusual happened in Ottawa, the Canadian capital. Office workers returning from their lunch breaks were surprised to feel the earth move beneath their feet and their office buildings tremble, causing pictures to fall from the walls and objects from desks.

People in the city immediately suspected an earthquake, though they are relatively rare in the region. As might be expected, reporters at newspapers in the city contacted Natural Resources Canada to find out what was going on. The journalists were surprised to discover that government seismologists told them they were unable to speak about it.

Meanwhile, the US Geological Survey was giving out plenty of information – a 5.5 magnitude quake had occurred at 1.41pm some 19km below ground on the Ontario-Quebec border.

One reporter hoping to find out more about the suspected earthquake was Tom Spears, a science reporter on the Ottawa →

→ Citizen newspaper. "The deputy minister's office issued a statement saying there was no information and it was not until after 6pm that we heard more."

A four-hour delay may not sound like much – but in a world increasingly driven by the internet and social media, it's a lifetime.

Spears says the delay is indicative of what some are calling censorship of the work carried out by scientists funded by the Canadian government. "The fastest way to find out information is to find out if they are working with America or with a university, because academics are still free to talk," says Spears.

He says that the earthquake incident is one of many cases where scientists funded by the Canadian government have been unable to share information on seemingly innocuous research.

A group of academics and students at the University of Ottawa organised a mock funeral to protest at what they saw as the death of scientific evidence in public policy making

"I can understand it if a scientist doing research that has enormous bearing on a sensitive area of public policy, if a bill is working its way through parliament for example, he is going to be sensitive about talking about it in public," says Spears. "What has been going on is the gagging of scientists over tiny little things."

In another case, Spears asked scientists working for Canada's National Research Council about work they were doing on snowfall. Spears says he was told by the organisation's communication chief that there would be no interview and that it would only provide a written statement.

So what are scientists allowed to say? The Canadian government has an official communications policy that was written in 2006 and updated in 2012. The policy states that government departments should "provide the public with timely, accurate, clear, objective and complete information about its policies, programs, services and initiatives" and "encourage public service managers and employees to communicate openly with the public about policies, programs, services and initiatives they are familiar with and for which they have responsibility".

However, it also makes clear that government employees should "treat sensitive information with discretion" and that "communication specialists responsible for media relations" should "ensure that media requests, particularly for interviews or technical information on specialised subjects" are "directed to knowledgeable managers or staff designated to speak as official representatives of their institution".

Communications professionals at Canada's government scientific organisations say that the problems in communicating science are not about censorship but more about timely access to commentators.

Charles Drouin, chief media relations officer for Canada's National Research Council, the country's major scientific research and development organisation, says that the snowfall research Spears was seeking was not being censored.

"That was an unfortunate incident," says Drouin. "The news went out on a smaller website and Tom Spears wanted to do a story within the next 24 hours and he approached us. We were ready to grant the interview and we wanted to make sure we gave access as quickly as possible. What didn't come out is that the researcher wasn't available on that day, he was in a conference and we asked if he could negotiate his deadline. But of course he wanted his story out the next day.

"Moving forward we will be clear when there is nobody available and we will try to negotiate. Our goal is to give access to scientists."

Drouin says that the NRC is dealing with an increasing number of media requests. He says the organisation handled 50 media requests in 2010 but that this had increased to 363 in 2012 and that 95 per cent of those requests for an interview do go ahead.

"The other 5 per cent is because there are sometimes confidentiality issues or licensing requirements and in other cases it is the unavailability of the spokesperson," he says.

He adds that it is sometimes the case that scientists themselves do not want to speak to reporters because they want to make sure the right message gets across.

According to Drouin the NRC uses government policy as a baseline, but works on a need-to-know basis. "Some of our researchers are well known to the media and they get approached directly but they usually let me know what is going on."

If this were only a case of one science reporter having his attempts at getting interviews with one government department fail, then you might argue that it was merely a difference of opinion or a personal vendetta. Yet these incidents are part of a larger and more worrying campaign that is increasingly looking like censorship of federally funded scientists by the Canadian government.

In early 2012, the presidents of six Canadian organisations representing government scientists and journalists sent an open letter on the issue to the Prime Minister Stephen Harper.

The letter said: "Despite promises that your majority government would follow principles of accountability and transparency, federal scientists in Canada are still not allowed to speak to reporters without the 'consent' of media relations officers. Delays in obtaining interviews are often unacceptable and journalists are routinely denied interviews. Increasingly, journalists have simply given up trying to access federal scientists, while scientists at work in federal departments are under undue pressure in an atmosphere dominated by political messaging...We urge your government to implement a policy of transparent and timely communication, one similar to that introduced in the US recently by the National Oceanic and Atmospheric Administration. This policy now encourages scientists to speak to the media without any intermediary. It even encourages scientists to express their own opinions, provided they indicate that they are speaking personally and not on behalf of the employer."

A few months later, a group of academics and students at the University of Ottawa organised a mock funeral to protest at what they saw as the death of scientific evidence in public policy making. One of the organisers, PhD biology student Katie Gibbs, said the event went "far better than we ever contemplated" and attracted several thousand people.

Gibbs says: "There had been a lot of cuts to science and restrictions on government scientists speaking about their research. In May 2012, the government put out a bill which modified dozens of pieces of legislation and there were lots of cuts to science programmes – the Experimental Lakes Area, a place that is known for its freshwater research, had its funding cut, for example. We felt that enough was enough, and if we didn't stand up for science, nobody was going to; we had to communicate to the public why this was such a problem.

"Prior to the event, there were stories of government scientists being muzzled and cuts to science funding and they were discussed as separate issues. The 'funeral' tied them together and put them in context for the general public."

In early 2013, Gibbs, along with some of the other organisers of the rally, established the pressure group Evidence for Democracy "to ensure that the best available scientific knowledge and evidence is used to inform decisions that affect the health and prosperity of Canadians". →

November
2007

Environment Canada implements guidelines requesting that scientists initially talk to journalists via media relations department

September
2010

Access to Information Act request by Canwest News reveals that Scott Dallimore, a geoscientist at Natural Resources Canada, was prevented from doing media interviews about his research on a 13,000-year-old flood published in Nature in April 2010

July
2011

Access to Information Act request by Canwest News reveals that Kristi Miller, a scientist at the Department of Fisheries and Oceans, had her work on salmon published in the prestigious journal Science but was not allowed to discuss her research publicly

March
2012

Presidents of six Canadian science organisations write open letter to government expressing concern at science communications policy

July
2012

Scientists hold mock funeral at the University of Ottawa to mark 'death of evidence' in government policy-making

October
2012

The Big Chill report reveals 90 per cent of government scientists feel they are unable to speak freely to the media about their work

Sources: www.scienceuncensored.ca, Evidence for Democracy

→ Gibbs says that the censorship of Canadian government science is part of a broad control of government communication. "The government has been very strong in controlling their message across the board. Some have described it as a broad muzzling that has caught science in its net. It is understandable in terms of politics but the desire to control has gone too far and to the point where it is harming our democracy.

"It really comes down to the fact that if the government has a mandate they want to implement then it is far easier if they don't have to worry about facts and evidence coming out."

Canada's censorship of scientists comes at a time when government-funded science is becoming more and more open. The internet has played an important role in this, allowing individuals to share information more easily and more widely than ever before.

Despite this, things do not appear to have improved in Canada.

In February 2013, the pressure group Democracy Watch asked Canada's information commissioner, Suzanne Legault, to investigate, under the provisions of the country's Access to Information Act, "the systematic efforts by the government of Canada to obstruct the right of the media – and through them, the Canadian public – to timely access to government scientists".

In a letter to the commissioner, the Environmental Law Clinic of the University of Victoria, said: "There are few issues more fundamental to democracy than the ability of the public to access scientific information produced by government scientists – information that their tax dollars have paid for. We as a society cannot make informed choices about critical issues if we are not fully informed about the facts."

At the time of writing, the commissioner had not yet ruled on the issue.

What is clear is that government scientists feel under threat when it comes to talking about their work.

In October 2013, the Professional Institute of the Public Service of Canada (PIPSC), the largest union in Canada representing scientists and professionals employed at the federal and some provincial and territorial levels of government, published a report, The Big Chill.

More than 4,000 scientists responded to a survey forming the core of the report and the findings underline concerns over censorship. It revealed that 90 per cent of respondents felt they were unable to speak freely to the media about their work.

More worryingly, for the Canadian public at least, only 14 per cent felt that if they knew of a departmental decision or action that, based on their scientific knowledge, could bring harm to the public interest, including to health, safety, or the environment, they felt able to share those concerns with the public or media without fear of censure or retaliation from their department or agency.

Two-thirds felt there had been a worsening of openness in recent times, with just under 75 per cent of those polled saying that sharing of government science findings with the Canadian public had become too restricted in the past five years.

Announcing the publication of the report, PIPSC president Gary Corbett said that Canadian federal scientists were facing "a climate of fear".

He said that there is "a chill brought on by government policies that serve no one's interests, least of all those of the Canadian public". He added: "The safety of our food, air, water, of hundreds of consumer and industrial products, and our environment depends on the ability of federal scientists to provide complete, unbiased, timely and accurate information to Canadians. Current policies must change to ensure these objectives are met."

The report concludes: "Canada's scientists deal primarily in facts. They are not known for ill-considered opinions or →

→ rash judgments. Sound policy, public awareness and the integrity of evidence-based decision-making require that science be heard. So when a clear majority of federal scientists state that they are not permitted to speak freely, that the sharing of scientific findings has become too restricted, that public policy has been compromised by political interference, and that greater protection for whistleblowers is needed, Canadians and government alike should listen."

And unlike the transitory tremors felt on that June afternoon in Ottawa in 2010, this one looks set to rumble on and on. X

Mark Frary is the author of eight books including How to Get a Sofa Around a Corner, Freaky Science and the Origins of the Universe for Dummies. He has written about science and technology for many publications including The Times. He is a member of the Association of British Science Writers. Before becoming a writer, he worked on the predecessor to the large hadron collider at the CERN nuclear physics laboratory and studied space plasmas at the Mullard space science laboratory. He tweets @markfrary

Blogging, blasphemy and bans

43(1): 119/122 | DOI: 10.1177/0306422014521737

Atheist bloggers in Bangladesh are fighting a battle for future freedoms, but against a harsh backdrop of attacks and legal action. **Salil Tripathi** reports

BEING A BLOGGER is dangerous these days in Bangladesh. One blogger has been murdered in the past year and four others now face trials under Bangladesh's strict laws against spreading communal hatred. This has been a period of significant political strife in Bangladesh; opposition parties boycotted the parliamentary elections held on 5 January 2013, which saw the ruling Awami League get re-elected. They won 232 out of 300 seats in an election marred by low turnout and violence.

The four bloggers on trial – Asif Mohiuddin, Subrata Adhikari Shuvo, Moshiur Rahman Biplob, and Rasel Parvez – are atheists who want to reduce the role of religion in the country's governance. They have been charged with blasphemy – specifically disseminating "false, indecent or defamatory" information and "hurting religious sentiments" under section 57 of the Information and Communication Technology Act of 2006. Anyone deliberately publishing, transmitting or causing to be published on a website, anything which is "fake and obscene" or could "deprave and corrupt" people, leading to deterioration of law and order, prejudice the image of the state, or hurt religious beliefs, can be charged. Offenders face imprisonment for up to 10 years.

The background to the bloggers' story starts in February 2012, when Abdul Quader Mullah, a leading politician of the Jamaat-e-Islami party, was convicted for war crimes committed during Bangladesh's war of independence in 1971. He was given a life term. Popular fury erupted; people congregated at Shahbagh in the centre of Dhaka and demanded a death sentence. The government amended laws and permitted the prosecutor to appeal, seeking a death sentence. The tribunal and the appeals court obliged. On 12 December 2013, Mullah was executed.

Back in February 2012, Rajib Haidar, a 30-year-old architect who was also a blogger and wrote seeking a ban on Jamaat's fundamentalist politics, which aims to make Bangladesh an Islamic state ruled by the shariah law, was stabbed to death. Haidar was a prominent activist in the Shahbagh movement.

The history behind this violence stretches back to Bangladesh's bloody war of independence. From 1947 to 1971 it was part of Pakistan, but Bangladesh sought it's freedom in 1971, which Pakistan tried to supress. As opposed to the majority of Bangladeshis, Jamaatis stood against independence. They supported the Pakistani Army, and now many of its leaders are implicated in war crimes that took place during the war of →

ABOVE: Hundreds of thousands of Islamists rallied in Dhaka after an overnight "long-march" to the Bangladeshi capital, demanding a blasphemy law and execution of "atheist bloggers" for defaming Islam

Credit: Palash Khan/Sipa USA/Rex

→ independence. It was only in 2008 that Jamaat's opposition, the Awami League, finally returned to power with a sufficiently large majority to establish an international war crimes tribunal. The Awami League, who fought for Bangladesh's independece during the war, had ruled briefly in independent Bangladesh's early years, but have been out of power for much of the past 40. The war crimes tribunal indicted 11 men, the majority of them from the Jamaat, sentencing all of them to death. Mullah was executed last December, even though international human rights groups have criticised the trials consistently as flawed; critics contend that the prosecution was routinely privileged over the defence, and unreliable evidence was accepted as fact.

So it was within this context that the Shahbagh stand-off was framed: in reality it was about those who sought accountability for war crimes and those who felt the Bangladesh should move on from the divisive past - that the politically motivated trials should stop. But the Jamaat skillfully described it as a conflict between the godless atheists on one side, and the devout and pious on the other.

As pro-tribunal activists laid siege at Shahbagh, anti-tribunal activists also converged in Dhaka. Nearly 100,000 activists belonging to Hefajat-e-Islam, a madrasa-based Islamic fundamentalist organisation, a large majority of them men, marched to Dhaka from Chittagong and elsewhere, seeking the death penalty for blasphemy and strong action against "atheist bloggers" (besides the four, the Hefajat has a list of another 80 bloggers it wants prosecuted). Such was the unfolding of events after the murder of Haidar, a supporter of the tribunal. Haider had launched a campaign on his blog demanding a ban on the Jamaat and calling for a boycott of its health, banking and other services. His killers have not yet been found, although his associates insist that Jamaat was involved. Jamaat has denied any responsibility.

The four bloggers currently facing trial are among several cases being prosecuted under Bangladesh's Information and Communication Technology Act. When they asked for the charges to be thrown out, police asserted that their "derogatory posts" (in which they opposed religion-based politics and sought a ban on the Jamaat) caused "a slide in law and order that led to anarchy." But, with internet penetration in Bangladesh estimated at as little as 6.3 per cent of the country's population, this accusation seems implausible.

Their trial was set for 6 November – but the prosecution did not produce any witness, and the trial was postponed to 4 March 2014. Meanwhile, the defence has filed four applications to quash the prosecutions. That case was to be heard on 8 December, but the court was unable to meet because of public unrest.

Bangladesh's laws against causing religious offence date back to the days of the British Raj – specifically to the criminal code introduced in 1860, just after the Indian war of independence of 1857 (known in Britain as "the mutiny"). Alarmed by how disparate Indian religions and groups had united to take on the might of the East India Company, the colonial administration decided to impose rules and laws that would ensure communal harmony, which meant not only that freedom of expression was curbed, but people were empowered to complain if they felt someone was jeopardizing communal harmony.

The law in Bangladesh – similar to India's – is that "outraging religious feelings" through "visible representation" or "attempts to insult religious beliefs" is punishable by up to two years imprisonment, with an extra year behind bars for anyone acting "with the deliberate intention of wounding the religions feelings" of another and "utters any word or makes any sound in the hearing of that person or makes any gesture in the sight of that person".

Men marched to Dhaka, seeking the death penalty for blasphemy and strong action against "atheist bloggers"

Bangladesh does offer constitutional protection to freedom of thought, conscience and speech. But the constitution also places "reasonable" restrictions on grounds of "interests of the security of the state, friendly relations with foreign states, public order, decency or morality, or in relation to contempt of court, defamation or incitement to an offence".

Mahbubul Rahman, who teaches law at Dhaka University, believes that criminal offences under the 2006 act are very loosely defined. He says in a legal note that, by expanding the definition, state power has been expanded, inflicting "unnecessary and precarious punishment". Rahman says that the ambiguity of the law creates "unlimited opportunity for state harassment and oppression". →

→ Bangladesh is living through charged times. The war crimes tribunal's verdicts have divided the population. Bangladesh's political culture is fragile, driven by two strong personalities – Prime Minister Hasina Wajed and former Prime Minister Khaleda Zia – leading rival parties, who see politics as a zero-sum game. Elections in January have not settled the issue. Once opposition parties boycotted the poll, the European Union and the United States did not send observers, and the government's credibility and legitimacy are being questioned. As many as 153 of the 300 seats were uncontested, and even with a low turnout and the opposition's boycott, the ruling party only won 79 of the 147 seats at play. The road ahead will be rocky.

In that volatile environment, freedom of expression will be at risk, as the bloggers' trial shows. In the grand scheme of things, Bangladesh has bigger problems to worry about. The sooner courts quash charges against the bloggers, the easier it will be for the state to diffuse tensions. ☒

Salil Tripathi is a London-based author, and is writing a book on the 1971 war

Legal eagle

43(1): 123/127 | DOI: 10.1177/0306422014523376

Former director of public prosecutions in England and Wales, and newly knighted, Sir Keir Starmer, discusses the right to offend, legal challenges for social media, and protection for whistleblowers, with Index editor **Rachael Jolley**

SIR KEIR STARMER is not one to dodge difficult challenges, or put his feet up. After all, he took on the post of director of public prosecutions (DPP) in England and Wales, overseeing the prosecution service, a job described by some as a "poisoned chalice". During his five-year term he appeared on television more often than previous holders of the post and helped raise awareness of the job. He also oversaw the establishment of new prosecution guidelines on the abuse of women and girls, the sexual abuse of children, and cases involving social media. Sir Keir is one of those incredibly bright people, who has the ability to discuss complex ideas, and get to the guts of them, using down-to-earth language that makes it possible for non-lawyers to understand. This is a skill that might equip him well for a change of direction, if, as has been mooted, he stands as a Labour member of parliament at the next UK election in 2015.

Sitting in the boardroom at his Doughty Street chambers, a large civil liberties and human rights practice, he is instantly relaxed, despite obvious demands on his time. On top of day-to-day cases, he has just taken on a brief from the UK opposition leader Ed Miliband to consider how victims and witnesses are interviewed during trials. At the same time he is preparing to join a post-conflict genocide investigation with the Croatian legal team at the International Court of Justice. As we walk past televisions showing a discussion on whether armed police officers should wear video cameras in the future, he comments "a good thing". "Even with the best will in the world, trying to remember events is fraught with difficulties."

We settle down to talk about another subject, but one he spent serious time on during his DPP term; considering new social media guidelines for the police, and the future role of social media in society. He believes there has not been enough political discussion about how outdated laws covering this area should be changed.

"The first thing to observe is there hasn't been a political debate about what the limits of free speech ought to be in this new era. There just hasn't been. There have been debates in the past about free speech and the criminal law or free speech and public order and they've led to very strong views on where the line ought to be drawn. But there hasn't even been the debate. So we're in a peculiar period."

He is concerned that the politicians don't appear to have this particular topic on their agenda, and they don't "have any appetite →

ABOVE: Sir Keir Starmer, while he was director of public prosecutions at the Crown Prosecution Service headquarters, London, March 2013

Credit: Rex

→ for it". He mentions, as he has done regularly in public, that in England and Wales the police fall back on the Communications Act 2003, which harks back to legislation designed in the 1930s to protect the sensibilities of operators putting calls through exchanges.

Does he feel new legislation is on its way? "I wouldn't expect it to be aired this side of an election and as far as I know none of the parties are shaping up to deal with it." He is convinced this problematic area of law needs more consideration. "I think we need to have an open debate about what the limits are. At the moment we're using out-dated legislation to try and deal with a new phenomenon."

The rise and rise of social media kicks off all sorts of questions, said Sir Keir. One of the ways we have judged language, debate and offence in the past is by where it is said; for instance, in the home, in the workplace or in a public space. That location had relevance to the number of people who would have heard the conversation. Now people can tweet or post from their back bedroom and the element of where you are when you make remarks makes little difference. Another factor is that people communicate on social media ~~in a~~ different way than they would do face to face; sometimes more openly, sometimes ruder, or franker, or perhaps more offensive. "So," said Sir Keir, "they take more risks, they use different language, and so that raises its own issues."

He added: "It is particularly challenging... because until now, broadly speaking, free speech has been governed by factors such as where you say it and what the reaction is. Hence, a lot of it is in the Public Order Act, which is where you wouldn't normally look for a free speech provision. But it was all about whether what you say disturbs public order and therefore, broadly speaking, you can say a lot more in your front living room than you can on the street. You can say a lot as long it doesn't cause people to want to engage in disorder, but not if it does. Now people have argued about whether that's right or wrong but that sort of balance has held for many years."

So where does that leave us? "The debate which is going to have to be resolved is, what's the right balance between the criminal law and free speech where social media is concerned? And this has barely begun."

Looking ahead, there are still some challenges, and Starmer, like most of us, is not sure how social media is going to look and be used in a decade's time, or what the impact of those changes might be.

"Where it will all end? I don't know, but I think there's no going back and therefore it is, on the face of it, open to anyone to self-broadcast in a way that was simply not available before. In the past, if you wanted to get your views known to hundreds of thousands of people, unless you used an established media outlet, it just wasn't going to happen, whereas now you can do it in your living room. There's no going back. I mean there is absolutely no going back."

Globally there are debates about the role of social media platforms in "policing" or taking down posts, as well as when that might or might not be necessary.

No one would suggest that platforms don't have any kind of role in what is "broadcast", says Starmer, and his test relates to the principle of harm. "If they [messages/tweets] are explicit and contain real threats to kill, or terrorist threats I don't think a service provider would do other than take them down very quickly. So anybody who says there is no responsibility, I think, is forgetting that in those circumstances I don't think any service provider would not take it down. It's what they do in the other situations."

As he points out, these platforms are operating globally, and the question is therefore whose laws, or social norms, do they adhere to? "Do you apply the test in the most restrictive country and apply it to everybody else and in that way make sure nobody's criminal law is ever breached, which means that we would all be subjective to very, very restrictive free speech provisions? Or do you go with the most generous, which means that national laws are likely to be breached on numerous occasions?"

I think when the whistle-blowing legislation is applied properly it works pretty well. It's people's perceptions of what protection it gives you or when it's misapplied that we get problems

He acknowledges that it is likely that there isn't going to be international criminal law developed in this area and, therefore, if there is going to be any criminal intervention it's going to be up to national law. So it's complicated when you are dealing with a global platform. "It does make life very difficult when you're talking about communications that spin across countries very, very quickly."

He adds: "There are international norms about certain types of conduct of →

→ behaviour, normally around mistreatment. It may be that over time international norms need to develop and that you could say that there is an emerging agreement that these are at least the outer limits of what ought to be freely available."

Despite being a strong advocate of free expression, not surprisingly, he doesn't believe in a society without laws, or complete freedom. "You can't have a law-free zone. Quite apart from threats of terrorism and real threats of violence, meaningful threats that are likely to be carried out, you have also court orders. What do you do about the anonymity of a rape victim? There are reasons why victims in these very sensitive cases are anonymised and if you simply

I am a very strong supporter of the Human Rights Act. I would not want to see is repealed or amended, but I would accept that there wasn't a big enough debate when it was first passed

say it doesn't matter that the court order is breached because you are using social media, you undermine the entire criminal justice system and you remove all the protection that's intended for very vulnerable victims."

Starmer was widely acknowledged as having helped install a culture of greater openness at the Crown Prosecution Service (CPS) while he was at its head. He agrees that the role changed while he was there: "I genuinely think and hope people would say the CPS is a much more open organisation now than it's ever been in the past. I think it's done it the world of good. I think people have more confidence in an organisation that explains itself more often."

He also believes that wider British society and its institutions have been going through a shift towards greater transparency, and towards a belief that it is important to explain decisions and debate them openly. "So to take my past role as director of public prosecutions, it was, in the past, perceived to be a bad thing if there was a public debate about whether the DPP got it right or wrong. Better not to have that debate than to have transparency and accountability, some thought. I fundamentally don't agree with that but I think we've moved way beyond that now."

And when the subject of whistleblowing comes up, we discuss whether in English law there is enough protection for people who choose to "out" information for the public good.

"I think when the whistleblowing legislation is applied properly it works pretty well. It's people's perceptions of what protection gives you or when it's misapplied that we get problems. I'm not saying the law couldn't be improved. You should always hold up these sort of laws and check whether they're working well in practice, but it is important that there is legal protection there and it's important that everybody appreciates it. I think a lot of people still labour under the misapprehension that if you whistle-blow you're necessarily engaging in wrongdoing and that it's something you can't do."

In this view there is, at the heart of society, a misunderstanding that if someone has broken a law to get some vital information into the public domain, they have necessarily done something wrong. "The only reason you protect whistleblowers is because they've got to do something wrong to get the information to where they believe it should be. Therefore, the argument that if someone has broken the law they are necessarily in the wrong is sterile."

The discussion of freedom of speech is often very different in Britain compared to, for example, the US, where schoolchildren learn about the first amendment as part of their history lessons, and where it is presented as at the heart of the nation's rights and self-image. So does Starmer believe the British need a written constitution and a First Amendment? "If you go to America [there] is a very, very strong sense that freedom of expression is a very important thing. We don't have this here, partly that's because of our history. I think if you have a common law system without positive rights it doesn't resonate in the same way. So you could only truly say that people had a positive right to freedom of expression when the Human Rights Act came along and that was 14 years ago when it actually came into force, in the year 2000."

Since the discussion of the Human Rights Act in the English, and to some extent British, media is highly emotional, and mostly negative, it is not surprising that Starmer recognises the public don't see it as a positive force, or understand what it covers. "I am a very strong supporter of the Human Rights Act. I would not want to see it repealed or amended but I would accept that there wasn't a big enough debate when it was first passed. I don't think people appreciate it, what this constitution and piece of legislation is really giving them."

His enthusiastic defence of the Human Rights Act has caught the attention of media commentators and put him head to head with the anti-human rights lobby in parts of the media. But he is clearly passionate about it. "I think the way that the European Convention is crafted and therefore the way the Human Rights Act is crafted is very clever. When you divide your rights into absolute rights and qualified rights, freedom of expression for me ought to be a qualified right. I don't accept the proposition that you can say what you like, when you like, without any limits at all. Having it as a qualified right under the convention, hence the Human Rights Act, seems to be a sensible approach where you can ...assert the right and then it's for whoever wants to restrict it to demonstrate why it should be restricted and then it's got to be necessary and proportionate. I think that's a perfectly good approach. I think it works very well, and I wouldn't want to disturb that approach."

When it comes down to it, he believes: "Freedom to simply say what other people want to hear is not that valuable and wouldn't be at all controversial, because nobody would restrict someone from saying something they wanted to hear. So freedom of expression only has bite when you're saying something which other people don't want to hear." ☒

@Rachael Jolley
www.indexoncensorship.org

Rachael Jolley in editor of Index on Censorship magazine

Brief biography

Sir Keir Starmer was director of public prosecutions in England and Wales from 2008-2013.

He was named QC of the Year in the field of human rights and public law in 2007 by the Chambers & Partners directory.

In 2005 he won the Bar Council's Sydney Elland Goldsmith award for his outstanding contribution to pro bono work in challenging the death penalty throughout the Caribbean.

From 2003-2008, Starmer was the human rights advisor to the Policing Board in Northern Ireland.

He has written several textbooks, including the Three Pillars of Liberty: Political Rights and Freedoms in the UK (1996), European Human Rights Law (1999), Criminal Justice, Police Powers and Human Rights (2001) and the Human Rights Manual and Sourcebook for Africa (2005).

He gave free advice to the defendants in the McLibel case.

Change your tune?

43(1): 128/131 | DOI: 10.1177/0306422014522939

Some homophobic lyrics in rap and reggae incite hatred and violence, agree campaigners **Peter Tatchell** and **Topher Campbell**. But is censorship the answer? First, Peter Tatchell explains why education will help. Then Topher Campbell tells **Alice Kirkland** where he would draw the line

ALONG WITH MISOGYNY, homophobic lyrics have long blighted some rap and reggae music. Eminem and Buju Banton, among others, have found themselves in the firing line for their incendiary anti-gay hate music, ranging from rap songs containing insults like "faggot" to tracks that overtly glorify and encourage the murder of lesbian, gay, bisexual and transgender people.

Homophobic hate speech is wrong, regardless of whether it is expressed by a bully in the street or by a singer. People are regularly prosecuted for racist insults but not for homophobic ones – at least not if they are big-name reggae and rap stars. No artist has, as far as I know, been arrested for singing or recording anti-gay hate songs. Is this a matter of double standards?

In 2004, together with the LGBT rights group OutRage!, the Black Gay Men's Advisory Group and J-Flag, the Jamaican LGBT rights movement, I launched the Stop Murder Music campaign. We campaigned for the cancellation of concerts by eight Jamaican reggae dancehall singers whose lyrics and public pronouncements incited the murder of LGBT people. They justified and encouraged the shooting, burning, hanging and drowning of "batty men". According to J-Flag, the release of these tracks coincided with a spike in homophobic violence. We did not oppose them because they were homophobic, but because they said LGBT people should be killed.

Police in Jamaica and the UK ignored calls for some singers to be prosecuted on charges of incitement to murder. In contrast, racist remarks – even ones that involve no violent threats – invariably result in a prosecution. Why is racist hate speech treated differently from homophobic hate speech?

When it comes to homophobia and other hate speech, I draw the line at incitement to violence. This is against the law – and rightly so. No one should be expected to live with violent threats. It intimidates the victim, making them afraid to speak out, thereby subverting and preventing free speech.

Incitement to homophobic hatred is now a crime, in line with racial and religious hatred. This is a bad move. As much as I deplore any form of hateful music, and believe it should be discouraged and condemned, it is not as bad as discrimination, harassment, threats or violence – all of which are qualitatively worse and are rightly criminalised. There is no need for separate legislation against hate speech.

ABOVE: Vybz Kartel, who had his MOBO nomination withdrawn in a row about homophobic lyrics

Credit: Everynight Images/Rex Features

Prolonged, extreme anti-gay hatred is potentially harmful to individuals, and anti-harassment laws are appropriate measures to combat this hatred.

One of the main problems with anti-hate laws is defining what constitutes hate. Unlike incitement to violence, hate is much more subjective. The line between hate speech and merely unpalatable viewpoints is hard to draw with certainty, clarity and consistency. This is also true when it comes to homophobic music. When does a bigoted rap song spill over into criminal hate speech? Who decides? How is hate defined?

Incitement to homophobic hatred is now a crime, in line with racial and religious hatred. This is a bad move. There is no need for separate legislation against hate speech

The state should not be given the power to decide on these matters, not least because these decisions are potentially open to abuse. →

→ In 2009, two anti-war protesters were prosecuted after they insulted British soldiers for their role in the Iraq war. They were convicted in 2011 on public order offences. Yet, for many, the protesters, who shouted insulting remarks at the crowd that had gathered to watch a military parade, were merely practising their right to free expression.

Christian street preachers have also been victims of over-zealous prosecutions. They have preached that homosexuality is immoral and that gay people will go to hell. I oppose their views, but I also oppose their prosecution.

Peaceful protests against hate speech have at times been criminalised, as if they themselves were a form of hate speech. In 1994, I was arrested for saying the homophobia and sexism of the Islamist extremist group

Criminalising intolerant and objectionable views is the slippery slope to censorship. At best it is a short term fix

Hizb ut Tahrir was akin to the bigotry of the Nazis. In another case, in 2008, a teenager was arrested for calling Scientology a dangerous cult. In both instances, it was deemed that our protests were insulting and had caused offence.

I don't believe that being spared offence is a human right. I'm offended by misogynistic clerics but I don't think they should be prosecuted for holding a viewpoint that I find detestable. Putting up with a degree of offence is the price we pay for a free and open society.

Free speech is one of the hallmarks of a democratic society. It should only be restricted in extreme circumstances. Criminalising intolerant and objectionable views is the slippery slope to censorship. At best, it is a short-term fix. It is also counter-productive. It risks making martyrs of people with bigoted opinions and deflects from the real solution to hate speech: information and debate to counter hateful ideas. A better solution is to promote education that rejects hateful ideas.

To "immunise" young people against homophobic lyrics and hate speech, education against all prejudice – including racism, sexism, homophobia and transphobia – should be a compulsory subject in every school; starting at primary level, with no opt-outs for independent, religious or free schools. Parents should not be given the right to withdraw their children. Lessons in equality and diversity will promote understanding and the acceptance of difference. Learning should include an annual examination, and results should be made available to future potential employers and educational establishments. This would ensure that pupils and teachers take these lessons seriously and would, over time, combat bigoted ideas, creating tolerance, respect and community cohesion. There would be no need for hate speech legislation.

People aren't born homophobic. They become homophobic. Education can prevent hate. Prevention is better than punishment. X

Peter Tatchell is a human rights campaigner: www. PeterTatchellFoundation.org

Homophobia in the music industry

Founder of Justice for Gay Africans and film critic ***Topher Campbell*** *talks to Index's* ***Alice Kirkland*** *about homophobia in the music industry*

Topher Campbell sees himself as someone who tells stories through his artistic work rather than as an activist. He announced he was gay to his friends when he was 15 and to his mother at the age of 20.

He recalls hearing music by artists such as Beenie Man and Vybz Kartel, two rappers notorious for their homophobic lyrics and their promotion of violence against the LBGT community, booming out of sound systems in some of London and New York's gay establishments.

Understanding the cultural context in which music is produced is crucial, and homophobic language doesn't feature only in black rap music, he says. He also believes that there can be a distinction between those who use terms like "batty boy" as homophobes – and those LGBT people who have begun to reclaim such words.

Like Peter Tatchell, Campbell draws a line at lyrics that promote violence against and even murder of LGBT people, but the idea of banning homophobic language in music does not sit well with him. As soon as something goes underground, he fears, resentment can result – ultimately generating more homophobia. "You also have to recognise that the history of banning black people is very emotive. I don't want to be banned from having relationships or from calling myself queer or gay."

He believes the music industry is inherently homophobic and is more concerned with selling records and maintaining images than worrying about the impact of words.

Increased awareness, more conversation and good education will help curb the use of abusive language in music, he says. "The cause and effect of words is very important, especially in the Twitter-infested, Facebook-dominated world we now live in. This is what most excites me: you can either go 'we'll ban all this stuff, it's really horrible and must be kept off social media' or you can find a way of understanding it, appreciating it, and changing it."

Campbell praises the Stop Murder Music campaign, a joint work of activism from several LGBT groups that ultimately led to the Reggae Compassionate Act, a declaration signed by several artists in 2007 following on a campaign led by gay rights group Outrage!. The act was signed by Baju Banton, Sizzla and Capleton, who had all previously released anti-gay tracks, as did Beenie Man.

But he feels that it wasn't until white campaigners came along that people really started to listen to the arguments about homophobic language in reggae and dancehall music.

There's a lot of racism in the gay scene, both in Britain and America, he says. This stems, Campbell thinks, from the privilege enjoyed by white gay men that sets the agenda for activism around the world. There's a mainstream respectable gay positioning which has absolutely nothing to do with the African-American experience, the black African experience or the black European experience. This has resulted in a narrative that does not take into account the culture of black societies, he says.

"I reject absolutely and whole-heartedly the idea of these big loud voices coming from Europe or America [and talking] about how the global south should live their lives and how music should happen."

Alice Kirkland is editorial intern at Index on Censorship

Give me liberty?

43(1): 133/135 | DOI: 10.1177/0306422013520279

The record of the devolved Scottish National Party government in Edinburgh suggests that an independent Scotland might not be a beacon for freedom of expression, warns **Padraig Reidy**

AS NEWS BROKE of the Clutha helicopter crash, a 16-year old Scottish boy sent the almost obligatory offensive tweet that follows all tragic news events.

It was yet another contribution to the mountain of pointless trolling tweets that are sent every day, usually by young men. But then the police got involved.

The boy was arrested and charged under the recently enacted Offensive Behaviour at Football and Threatening Communications (Scotland) Act.

That was bad enough, you'd have thought. But Lord Advocate Frank Mulholland, Scotland's chief legal officer, would disagree with you. According to the Herald newspaper, he advised procurators fiscal (public prosecutors) that "where it can be demonstrated an offence was motivated by a reaction to events at the Clutha, there will be a presumption in favour of criminal proceedings".

The Herald welcomed the Lord Advocate's advice, stating in an editorial: "The internet should be a place of free expression but it should not be a place that is free from the law. Those who do not realise that should be met with a policy of zero tolerance until the culture catches up with the law."

Mulholland's statement came just weeks after the Scottish National Party government issued its blueprint for an independent Scotland. As Scotsman columnist Alex Massie despairingly tweeted: "The new Scotland, don't you know."

The SNP document, Scotland's Future, doesn't really mention free speech. But recent legislation does not inspire a huge amount of confidence in an independent Scotland's commitment to freedom.

Discussions about speech laws in Scotland have largely concerned the sectarian divide between Protestants and Catholics that has blighted the country.

Until the demotion of Rangers football club to Scotland's lowest league in 2012, punishment for years of financial mismanagement, "Old Firm" matches between Rangers and their Glasgow rivals Celtic were pretty much the highlight of a top-flight domestic football season that had long since stopped being competitive. The clubs dwarfed the other teams in the Scottish Premier League, in terms of money, success and influence.

The Old Firm matches come with a history of antagonism. Celtic is seen as the team of immigrant Irish Catholics, while Rangers is the team of lowland Scots Protestants. Exacerbated by the sectarian conflict in Northern Ireland, the rivalry has long been a hotbed of bitterness and abuse. →

ABOVE: Scotland's First Minister and Scottish National Party (SNP) leader Alex Salmond smiles after delivering his keynote speech at the party's annual conference in Perth, Scotland October 2012

→ "The Famine Song" is an example of a song that Rangers fans would sing about Celtic fans. Referring to the Irish potato famine of the mid-19th century, which caused huge numbers of Irish people to leave the country (some finishing up in Glasgow), the song's pretty uninspired lyrics played on various anti-Catholic tropes, dotted with the catchy refrain "The famine's over, why don't you go home?" In 2008, it gained notoriety when the Irish consulate in Glasgow formally complained about its use, and in 2009 a man was successfully prosecuted for singing it. But that was not the end of the issue.

Studies suggested that public order breaches and incidents of domestic violence increased sharply on the days of Old Firm matches. The solution was proposed that in order to dampen the tensions on matchdays, the "Up The 'RA!"/"Fuck The Pope!" songs be criminalised.

The Offensive Behaviour at Football and Threatening Communications Act aimed to curb sectarian and abusive chanting at Old Firm games, where nominally Catholic, Irish republican Celtic fans would sing songs about praising the IRA, and nominally Protestant, Ulster loyalist Rangers fans would sing anti-Catholic and anti-Irish songs.

It is, by all accounts, a dreadful piece of legislation. Indeed, one sheriff (judge), dismissing a case, went so far in describing the act as to say: "Somehow the word mince comes to mind."

But now this particular dog's dinner is already being used beyond its original purpose, which was to attempt to quell matchday tensions. The fact that this is the first major piece of legislation affecting speech brought in under an SNP government (and an independent Scotland would, presumably,

Credit: David Moir/Reuters

have an SNP government at least in its early years) does not bode well.

There have been other worrying signs of Scotland's possible direction when it comes to future free-expression issues.

On 29 November 2012, the day Lord Justice Leveson announced the findings of his inquiry into the "culture, standards and ethics" of the press, Scotland's first minister, Alex Salmond, announced that Scotland would have an expert group look into the report and make its own recommendations.

The report of the Expert Group on the Leveson Report in Scotland was published in March 2013. The group, led by Lord McCluskey, a former solicitor general, did not depart hugely from any of Lord Justice Leveson's recommendations – except on one key, and quite alarming, point.

Leveson, in an admittedly muddled way, had attempted to retain voluntary status for a regulator, and differentiate between the traditional business of newspapers and other, newer, publishing models.

But McCluskey's men were not convinced of this distinction. They stated: "There is no practical alternative to making it compulsory for all news-related publishers to be subject to the new system of regulation. It appears to us that the Leveson approach was predicated on the hope that most – or even all – significant news publishers would join the new system voluntarily. But on that approach, if significant news publishers declined to join there would be no mechanism to compel them to do so."

Alarmingly, they went on to suggest that any Scottish regulator would have to include social media, a step too far for the first minister.

"Alex Salmond ain't stupid, so thanked the commissioners for their hard work and filed it under 'too hot to handle'," David Torrance, author of an autobiography of Salmond, told Index.

He went on: "Last time I heard, Scottish government officials were simply suggesting tweaks to the UK Royal Charter, so it's quite a climbdown from the original posture. But press regulation is fully devolved, so they can do what they want."

So is there any hope at all for Scotland becoming a beacon of free speech? Gerry Hassan, author of Caledonian Dreaming: The Quest for a Different Scotland,

The Offensive Behaviour at Football and Threatening Communications Act is already being used beyond its original purpose, which was to attempt to quell match-day tensions

suggested to Index that, freed from the constraints of Eurosceptic feeling in Westminster, Scotland could talk more positively about the right to free speech enshrined in the European Convention. But even then, he warned against the dangers of being seen to be doing something, as evidenced by the Offensive Behaviour at Football law.

So the question still looms: will an independent Scotland be a free Scotland? ☒

Padraig Reidy is a senior writer at Index on Censorship

Secret signals

43(1): 136/139 | DOI: 10.1177/0306422014521759

Underground journals smuggled from house to house during the Communist era in `the Soviet Union became one of the few ways of reading independent news. In authoritarian Belarus, they are still a force today. Journalist **Andrei Aliaksandrau** reports

SAMIZDAT IS ONE of the Russian words brought to the world through the events of the turbulent 20th century. "Self-publishing", as samizdat can literally be translated as, has a long history and is still a reality in one post-Soviet country, Belarus. The USSR might be history now, but remnants of its attitudes can still be found throughout the post-Soviet region, shaping its mentality, governance, and its political and economic development. Samizdat has survived as well. In Belarus, a part of the former Soviet empire, underground publications are still very much a part of the media landscape.

Ales (not his real name) was an Belarussian activist who belonged to an opposition youth movement. He worked as a "postman". He did not deliver letters or parcels, he was part of a clandestine distribution network for an unregistered newspaper.

It was a weekly newspaper, produced by an editorial board of professional journalists and editors, who wrote about corruption among authorities; political prisoners; and the real reasons for the political and economic crises Belarus has gone through under the rule of Alexander Lukashenko, a man who has occupied the post of president of the country since 1994, and does not want to leave it.

Every Friday Ales got a call from a man. He only knew his name, and recognised the mobile number. Ales confirmed he was at home, and in an hour or so his doorbell rang. There was the man with a bag of freshly printed newspapers. There were more than a thousand copies, eight pages of A4. The man greeted Ales, gave him the newspapers and left. They barely knew each other, and never met outside that "conspiracy".

Ales's job was to fold the newspapers, put them into envelopes and then mail them to subscribers. These were people, who had informed the editorial board either through a network of local activists or by contacting a secure mobile phone number registered in Lithuania, that they wanted to receive the paper regularly.

Ales finished stuffing the envelopes, and then went out onto the streets of Minsk to post them. He did not use the same mailbox every time. He only had 200-250 envelopes with him at any one time, and not just for logistical reasons: every publication with a circulation of more than 300 copies has to be officially registered in Belarus and it is a crime to "act on behalf of an unregistered organisation". Ales travelled to another district of the Belarusian capital, put the batch of envelopes with the newspaper in a mailbox in front of a post office and went home to get another batch to post somewhere else.

There are about 30 to 40 unregistered newspapers and bulletins that are still published all over Belarus. They cover local news state-run newspapers don't cover. Some of them are dedicated to issues of human rights, youth initiatives, or local history and national culture.

"These publications not only provide people with information, they are also a powerful tool for keeping activists together. They help local civil society activists to attract new members to their initiatives through publishing a local bulletin," said Rodger Potocki, senior director, Europe, at the National Endowment for Democracy.

Modern technologies affect the way today's samizdat is produced. Most underground newspapers are printed on Risograph machines and some of them are designed quite professionally, but it is also possible now to distribute them in different ways.

Aliaksandr Starykevich, the editor of Salidarnasc newspaper, says: "We produce a weekly publication in a PDF format, and put it on a special section of our website. It is quite popular with local branches of independent trade unions: they just download the publication and print it out for their members. Its paper version was suspended because of pressure from the authorities, and it now only exists as an online publication (www.gazetaby.com) and a PDF bulletin."

Starykevich, who is also vice-chairman of the Belarusian Association of Journalists, says it is the media situation that allows samizdat publications to exist and be in demand among the population in Belarus.

He said: "We have a record number of Soviet rarities which still exist in our country. For example, there is a modern version of Pravda newspaper, still called The Soviet Byelorussia (Sovetskaya Belorussiya) and published by the presidential administration. The existence of semi-clandestine publications shows traditional media cannot satisfy the audience's need for information. We have 118 administrative districts in Belarus,

ABOVE: Copies of samizdat newspaper Chronicles of Current Events displayed in the museum of Sakharov Centre in Moscow

Credit: Valeriya Sauchankava

but only a dozen of them have independent newspapers."

Forty-five years ago, in August 1968, the Soviet army occupied Czechoslovakia to suppress the anti-Communist uprising that had taken place in the country. On 25 August 1968, seven Soviet dissidents went out to Red Square in Moscow to protest against the occupation and express their support for rebellious Prague. They were arrested and later tried. Those who read the Soviet press had no opportunity to learn about their actions. Vague, propaganda-style reports about the sentence depicted members of the group as drunkards, spongers and →

ABOVE: Belarusians struggle to find out all the news they want to know

→ profligates, who hated their Soviet motherland. Their picket was presented as an act of hooliganism and debauchery, and the reason for it went unmentioned.

Yet, many Soviet citizens were able to learn about the story. They did not hear about it from state TV, or by reading about it in Pravda, of course. Their source of information was samizdat, small-circulation newspapers and bulletins, published in semi-clandestine conditions and passed from reader to reader.

Chronicles of Current Events stands out from a list of samizdat publications because it was first ever human rights bulletin published in the Soviet Union. It was launched in 1968, the same year the Soviet tanks rolled through the streets of Prague.

Leonard Ternovsky, a Soviet doctor, writer and human rights activist, wrote, in his book about the Chronicles: "I must admit at the very beginning I would not have singled out the Chronicles of Current Events from a set of samizdat publications that were passed from hand to hand at that time. But soon I realised those pieces of paper would lead to serious trouble. The Soviet authorities would severely punish anyone found reading them, and the people who distributed them among their friends, but they would leave those who

Credit: photo.bymedia.net

actually wrote and produced them alone. It did not take long for me to become an ardent admirer of this publication. Every time I read it I passed it to my friends, and could not wait for the next issue."

First, the bulletin was published quite regularly, about once every two months. It had a set of regular editorial sections, with a short overview of the latest events, arrests of dissidents, searches of their homes, news about political prisoners in Soviet jails and labour camps as well as facts about the persecution of religious and ethnic minorities in the USSR. It also contained a review of other samizdat publications, poems or stories by blacklisted authors, plus historical documents that proved the brutality of the Soviet regime. The style of articles was quite fact-based, tight, and sometimes even a bit cold, but this was because of the way the Chronicles were actually produced.

Liudmila Alexeeva, one of the founders and current chairman of the Moscow Helsinki Group, was one of the people who actually typed the bulletin and helped distribute it in a viral way.

"I usually received the first draft copy from the editor and produced the first copies, and then they were re-typed by other people, who had typewriters, seven or eight copies each. I have always cherished freedom of expression, starting from the time of the Soviet Union, when, first of all, I wanted to hear or read what others had to say about the issues that were important to me. Because of severe censorship, it wasn't easy. That's why I became a strong supporter of samizdat. I learned to type to help distribute the Chronicles of Current Events. This publication by the defenders of human rights in Moscow became an embodiment of free speech to me."

Despite a real danger of persecution, the editorial team of the Chronicles asked their readers for feedback and information.

The fifth issue of the publication stated: "Everyone who is interested in Soviet society knows what is going on in their country and can provide the Chronicles with information. Tell it to the person you got the bulletin from, he will tell it to the one he got it from. Do not try to go down the whole chain yourself – or we will consider you an informer,"

In 1972 the bulletin was temporally suspended as the KGB started to put pressure on the dissidents. It was later restored, and published until November 1983, when Yury Shikhanovich, one of the editors of the Chronicles, was arrested. Liudmila Alexeeva had to leave the country. Several authors of the bulletin, like Shikhanovich or Sergey Kovaliov, served terms in prison, labour camps or internal exile. They were released when Perestroika brought the wind of change to central and eastern Europe.

The Soviet authorities would severely punish anyone found reading them, and the people who distributed them

Today, the internet is undoubtedly becoming a more and more important source of information for Belarusians, a way for them to get a variety of news. But with coverage still only around 50 per cent and even less in the provinces, it's vital to find other ways of getting information to large groups of people. That's why modern versions of the Chronicles of Current Events, which hark back to the traditional Soviet-era samizdat, are still very much in demand.

Andrei Aliaksandrau is Belarus and OSCE programme officer at Index, and a Belarusian journalist

Thinking allowed

43(1): 140/144 | DOI: 10.1177/0306422014522943

Philosopher **Julian Baggini** takes a journey around political oppression to discuss free will with those who have experienced political restrictions on their freedoms

CHOOSING WHAT TO eat from a menu is hardly the highest expression of human freedom. Yet the restaurant Ognisko, in the affluent Kensington district of London, has a special role in Europe's history of political liberty. It is part of the Polish Hearth Club, founded in 1940 as a centre for Poles exiled from their home country after the Nazi invasion. It continued this role throughout the Cold War and now remains a centre for the capital's Polish community.

It was, therefore, a fitting venue for a discussion with a group of people who have all experienced a lack of political freedom. But it would not be at all suitable for most Anglophone philosophers who ponder freedom of the will, for whom that issue is entirely distinct. Political freedom concerns the structures of society that prevent us from, or enable us to, believe what we want, say what we want and do what we want. Free will is the capacity all humans may or may not have to make such choices freely in the first place. If, for example, you think that all our choices are determined by our genes, then you may conclude no one has free will, whether they live in North Korea or South Dakota.

It would seem therefore that political freedom and free will ("metaphysical freedom") are just two different things, and that one sheds no light on the other. I'm not convinced this rigid separation is right, however, and my Polish lunch was an attempt to dig a little deeper and discover what, if anything, the insights of those who have experienced deprivations of political liberty could contribute to our understanding of free will.

Around the table were Andrei Aliaksandrau, a journalist from Belarus, which, as he says, is "known as the last true dictatorship in Europe"; the journalist Ismail Einashe, the son of a Somali anti-government activist during the time of his country's dictatorship, who came as a refugee to Britain when he was ten years old; Rahela Sidiqi, a women's and human rights' activist who lived in Afghanistan under the Taliban; and Ma Jian, a Chinese novelist whose books have been banned in his home country. All are now based in Britain.

Listening to their stories, it seems to me that they all concern ways in which the structures of society erect obstacles to the exercise of free will. For instance, Sidiqi believes that we are here in this world to help humanity. But "God never puts you in chains if you don't do it. He leaves it to yourself." Her political ideal is that "human beings would be free in [a] way that God has created us," and that certainly wasn't the case in Afghanistan under the Taliban.

Aliaksandrau also talks of restrictions on freedom in terms of blocks. Alexander →

ABOVE: Cartoon of Jean-Paul Satre, French philosopher and free will theorist

Credit: Mary Evans/Jeffrey Morgan Collection/Reuters

→ Lukashenko has been president of Belarus for twenty years, and although his regime is not as brutal as some dictatorships, people have been kidnapped and killed, and there are political prisoners. "All political rights are quite restricted," says Aliaksandrau. "Journalists and social activists are blocked from fulfilling their duties, working freely and speaking freely."

This illustrates the most straightforward link between political and metaphysical freedom: free will involves the capacity to do certain things by our own volition, and the right political structures need to be in place in order for you to express those capacities. Political freedom is thus the external condition of fully expressing an internal capacity we all have.

However, if you push this idea a little further, I think you can see how those internal

Free will involves the capacity to do certain things by our own volition, and the right political structures need to be in place in order for you to express those capacities

capacities are not just there, whether we are able to express them or not. Political structures can actually affect how much free will we have, since it is deeply tied up with our natures as social beings, embedded in particular cultures and times.

Take, for instance, the capacity to make political choices, expressed most obviously at the ballot box. "Back in 2010 when I was in Somaliland for the general election," says Einashe, "a lot of people were queuing up the in villages, going to vote. You could say they were exercising their freedom there, but the majority of them were illiterate, so were they making an informed choice? If you don't have equality and education, how can they possibly be informed? If people don't have the education and the economic means, how can they ultimately determine things for themselves?" Similarly, Sadiqi believes that when women in rural Afghanistan choose to cover their faces they are not usually acting under a condition of freedom, because the alternative is not a "live" option in their communities. A person who is more informed and educated has more capacity to make choices for herself, and therefore has a more developed free will.

This idea of free will as being a matter of degree challenges the usual assumption that it is a capacity we do or do not have. Unlike say, cats, humans can not only do what they want, they can ponder their own wants, question their own preferences. But we can't all do this to the same extent. If we have no access to education and rely on information passed on to us by those with more power, we do not have as much of this freedom as we might. So there is a sense here in which an absence of political freedom can limit our freedom of thought, deliberation and choice. The political limits the personal, and the public conditions the private.

The other side of this coin is that even if the political structures of society allow you to exercise your capacities of free will, that doesn't necessarily mean you will. That's why the table gave a collective sigh and a nod when I asked whether they thought people in Britain did not take full advantage of their opportunities to exercise their freedom. "They were born into democracy, they never had to fight for it, and they take it for granted and they just don't value anything that is given to them for free which they don't pay personally for," says Aliaksandrau.

Jean-Paul Sartre made an even stronger claim when he wrote that the French were "never more free than during the German occupation". How could this be so? "Because the Nazi venom seeped even into our thoughts," he argued, "every accurate thought was a conquest. Because an all-powerful police tried to force us to hold our tongues, every word took on the value of a declaration of principles."

For those in our lunch party, this was putting it too strongly. "I don't believe you become freer when you're oppressed," said Ma Jian. "Look at North Korea. When you say I don't have the freedom to go back to China, you cannot invert that and say I have the freedom not to go to China."

Aliaksandrau also takes issue with Sartre. "You don't become freer when you are oppressed but you start really appreciating freedoms when they're under threat or when you actually lose them. The declaration of human rights was adopted after the Second World War when the whole of humanity saw what it is like when you don't have freedom and you don't have rights and people were terrified with what happened. Unfortunately, human beings need tragedy to start thinking."

I agree that Sartre is somewhat hyperbolic in his claim. But he is on to something, namely that to be truly free as a human being requires more than the absence of constraint. You have to use your own capacity to make choices, and accept responsibility for your own decisions. In that sense, it is indeed possible to become more acutely aware that you do have fundamental choices to make when restrictions are placed on them, and you can let your free will muscle entropy when things become easy.

But there is nothing about living under oppression which automatically makes one more aware of one's freedom. People can take oppression as much for granted as they do freedom. "It's like the rules of the game," says Aliaksandrau. "It's so naturally a part of your life that you can just go on with it."

Where Sartre goes most fundamentally wrong is in thinking that real free will is in a sense entirely a matter of attitude, distinct from the situation in the world. Rather than separating political and metaphysical freedom, however, I think we should see true freedom as requiring both. The most free person both fully utilises his or her own capacities of choice and deliberation, and is not excessively constrained by society. When either of these conditions is absent, our freedom is diminished; if neither are fulfilled, we have none at all.

Ma Jian sees society sapping individuals' free will when he looks at the work of writers who have remained in China and have, in sometimes subtle ways, altered their writing as a result. "I would become like them if I went back. That would be terrible." This highlights one of the most sinister aspects of totalitarian societies: their capacities to mould our ways of thinking in ways we are not even aware of. "It's like a shadow, like brainwashing, you don't even see it," he says.

They were born into democracy, they never had to fight for it, and they take it for granted.

There is another aspect of received opinion about free will that our discussion challenged. Paradigmatic examples of free will in the philosophical literature often centre around simple choices. You opt for *barszcz*, the famous beetroot soup, but you could have picked *trzaski*, crispy pork crackling, instead. The emphasis here is on the ability to do other than what you actually do. "Could have done otherwise" is pretty much the definition of a free choice.

And yet when you look at standing up for political freedom, it more often looks like a case of could *not* have done otherwise. Sidiqi, for example, stands up for women's rights. But surely she does not feel that rejecting them is an option and she agrees there is a sense in which she feels she must stick by them. →

→ Similarly, Aliaksandrau says "For me, when we talk about political freedoms, it's not even a choice, it's the only natural thing. I can't think, shall I go to thinking that freedom of expression is very bad? No! It's not even an option." The most meaningful choices are often the ones that we feel we must make, in order to retain our integrity. Free choices can thus be in one way compelled.

Freedom is not the ability to just choose anything. To be free is to able express one's fundamental values, to live according to the identity one has. And yet these values and these identities are not things we choose in any straightforward way. "If I'm honest," says Einashe, "most of my life has been spent living a life defined by culture and by faith that I didn't choose." Of course these things do not set our identities and values in stone. "Much of my own personal struggle has been choosing myself to have the choice to say that I could be secular, I could be humanist, I could be liberal," he says. But such struggles do not start from a clean slate. We make our choices from within situations that we did not choose, asserting values we acquired and which we often feel force themselves upon us. "We cannot segregate free will from the wider context of the influence of others and the environment," as Sadiqi put it.

Aliaksandrau summed it up well. "Pure free will does not exist because of all the influences we get throughout life, even because we're born in this particular country, in this particular century, with these particular parents. There are things that we're not really choosing."

Indeed, it is because being able to express one's unchosen identity is such an important freedom that the inability to live or work in your country of origin can be so painful. "In exile, free will cannot exist," says Ma Jian. "Free will is impossible when one is denied the freedom to return to one's homeland." When your passport is taken, something of you is taken too. You are not complete, and cannot express yourself fully. "Being a national of a country or being part of a nation is such a part of your identity that living in exile restricts your identity in some way," as Aliaksandrau puts it.

Our conversation bolstered my conviction that political and metaphysical freedom are parts of the same whole, not distinct capacities. If that's right, then it also supports the view that free will is not something either present or absent, but something we have in degrees. You build your freedom step by step, and you may overcome one barrier to freedom – political, social, economic, educational, psychological, historical – only to encounter another one. As Aliaksandrau put it, "It's not a state, it's a process." X

Julian Baggini is author of The Virtues of the Table, and is writing a new book on the philosophy of free will, which will be published next year

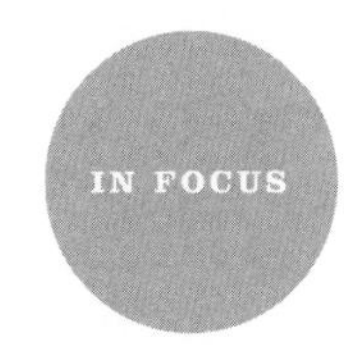

The beautiful game?

43(1): 145/147 | DOI: 10.1177/0306422014522940

There's little evidence of anti-semitism in English football right now, but vigilance is still needed, says **Anthony Clavane**

FIRST OF ALL there was the "Y-word debate", in which London's Tottenham Hotspur fans were criticised for continuing to use the term "Yid Army" to describe themselves. Spurs, who are viewed as a Jewish club, have, over the years, become the target of anti-semitic abuse from other teams' supporters. They argue that they have reclaimed the word. Still, the English Football Association deemed that they were using a racist term and threatened to prosecute any Tottenham fan joining in with the chant. It became, for some, a freedom of speech issue and, as a football reporter, I have attended many games in which fans of the north London club sing, defiantly, "We're Tottenham Hostpur, we sing what we want."

Personally, as a Jew, I find the Y-word offensive. It's as bad as the N-word being applied to black people and the P-word used against Asians. I accept the argument that it has been reclaimed – although those who chant it are mostly non-Jewish – and that the intent is positive. It's the same argument, I suppose, as gay people reappropriating the word "queer". Less complicated, however, is Nicolas Anelka's *quenelle* gesture. Last month, the French striker celebrated the first of his two West Brom goals with his right arm extended towards the ground, palm opened, and the other one bent across his chest touching his right upper arm. The gesture had not been seen by many journalists at the game but had been picked up by the cameras and instantly condemned by tweeters watching it in France. According to The Independent's French correspondent, John Lichfield, it "appears to merge the Nazi salute with a traditional, obscene French insulting hand signal, the *bras d'honneur*, which means, roughly speaking, 'up yours'."

The gesture is not about freedom of expression. It is about showing solidarity – as the footballer argued – with his "persecuted" comedian friend, Dieudonné M'bala M'bala, the man who invented the salute. In his stage shows, Dieudonné has insulted the memory of Shoah victims, given a platform to Holocaust deniers and promoted all kinds of Jew-hatred. And yet he has somehow become the poster boy not just of the far right but also sections of the anti-establishment left. Despite several convictions for racism – and most recently, in a notorious riposte to a critic, declaring "When I hear Patrick Cohen speak, I think to myself 'gas chambers, too bad'" – his anti-semitic discourse has struck a chord with a diverse constituency of radical Islamists, hip middle-class white Parisians, young people of foreign descent and Jewish-world-domination conspiracy theorists. "Look at the composition of Dieudonné's audiences," says French football writer Philippe Auclair. "There are people from the far right, but also people from the far left. People on →

ABOVE: West Bromwich Albion's Nicholas Anelka makes the *quenelle* gesture after scoring his first goal during a match against West Ham in December 2013

Credit: John Walton/EMPICS Sport/Press Association

> → **Dieudonné has given a platform to Holocaust deniers – yet has become the poster boy not just of the far right but also sections of the anti-establishment left**

the margins. There are Green extremists and radical Muslims. There is this unfocused anti-globalisation movement which talks about the US-Zionist conspiracy. To them, if the English Football Association clamp down on Anelka and give him a long ban it will be proof that American-Zionists control the FA. Some of the people tweeting me, for example, have pointed out that the FA's previous chairman was called Bernstein."

David Bernstein's predecessor at the FA, Lord Triesman, also happens to be Jewish. I interviewed both Triesman and Bernstein for my book Does Your Rabbi Know You're Here?, about Jewish involvement in football, and both men – who were at the forefront of anti-racist initiatives at the FA – told me that English football does not have a "Jewish problem". In my experience, as a fan, reporter and writer of two books on the subject, I can confirm that anti-semitism has all but disappeared from stadiums. But, unless we are vigilant, the *quenelle* controversy could be a way for it to return.

For example, what if the next time Anelka's team, West Bromwich Albion, play Spurs and the Albion fans make the salute against the "Jewish" club Spurs in support of Anelka? Then, in retaliation, Spurs supporters sing the "Y-word" back at them? Do we say to Jewish fans, watching on television, this is a price that has to be paid for freedom of speech? Of course not. Just as black people should not have to hear monkey chants at a soccer ground, Jewish fans should not be subject to anti-semitic chanting.

Anelka, of course, claimed he was merely being "anti-establishment". And a poll in Le Point magazine revealed that 77 per cent of French people were not offended by the *quenelle*. "Anybody," noted Nabila Ramdani in The National, "from schoolchildren to celebrities and politicians, could and did perform (the gesture) during those goofing around moments which are nowadays invariably caught on smart phone cameras." Ramdani added: "There is absolutely no question that Anelka would condemn the revolting pictures of idiots performing quenelles outside Holocaust memorials, or other sites marking attacks on Jews."

This so-called "anti-establishmentism" is anti-semitism by another name. It argues, like the Nazis did, that "the Jews" pull the strings, and are bent on promoting their "agenda" in the media – which, naturally, they control. Nobody has the right to racially abuse black players in football these days – nor should they have the right to spread this vile anti-Jewish racism.

Defenders of freedom of speech should, in my view, never support those who spout, or deliberately provoke, racism. Just as they wouldn't, I imagine, support those who shout "fire" in a crowded room. Those liberals and progressives who have championed Anelka's right to use the *quenelle* are, at best, misguided and, at worst, giving a platform to a conspiracy theory of power which insists that "the Jews" are bent on some grand plan of world domination. They are, in short, flirting with anti-semitism. ☒

For an alternative view, read Padraig Reidy on Index on Censorship's website at http://bit.ly/1ktbPvi

Note
A previous version of this story wrongly said that Nabila Ramdani had omitted to mention the use of the quenelle outside Holocaust memorials.

Anthony Clavane is a senior sports writer at the Sunday Mirror, and author of Promised Land and Does Your Rabbi Know You're Here? His latest play is Playing the Joker

Lights, camera, cut

43(1): 148/152 | DOI: 10.1177/0306422013519892

For years, Beijing has defied calls to stop censoring films and adopt a ratings system. **Tom Fearon** reports on the fine line Chinese directors and screenwriters tread to balance artistic integrity and profitability

FOR MORE THAN 60 years, China's Communist rulers have used cinema as a medium to carry their message, seeing its role as a commercial enterprise as less important. And for many years, one of the government's most effective means of controlling what is left on the cutting room floor has been its refusal to introduce a film ratings system.

As the world's fastest-growing movie market and the largest film industry outside the United States, China's growth in this area has been nothing short of blockbuster proportion. In 2013, box office spending hit more than US$3 billion, up 35 per cent year on year. Over the past decade, the number of cinemas in the country has grown tenfold, reaching more than 13,000. Open-air theatres that once screened grainy revolutionary films have been replaced by modern multiplexes, where urbanites don't balk at paying 180 yuan (US$30) for the latest 3D blockbuster, even if it's missing a few scenes or a few new ones, shot in China, have been added.

In early 1998, James Cameron's blockbuster Titanic flickered to a small yet powerful audience in the projection room of the China Film Group's Beijing headquarters. Seated in the middle was the country's then president Jiang Zemin who, at the urging of his propaganda chief, had been tasked with deciding if the movie in its uncensored form could sail into Chinese theatres.

The movie's climax that night wasn't when Leonardo DiCaprio slipped to his watery grave or even when the ship plunged into an iceberg; it unfolded as Kate Winslet posed naked for her portrait.

Jimmy Wu, then general manager of Paramount-Universal joint venture United Cinemas International, fought to keep the scene despite orders from the State Administration of Radio, Film and Television (SARFT), China's main censorship body to axe it.

"I explained how the portrait was critical to the story, and how if the scene was cut the audience wouldn't understand where it had come from," recalled Wu, today the chairman of cinema investment company Lumière Pavilions.

Frustrated and wary of blowback from Hollywood, Wu called the state council's propaganda chief, a bridge partner and close associate of his uncle, who after some wrangling arranged a private screening for Jiang to decide if the film in its original form was shipshape. The president gave it his nod, but the nude scene was cut 15 years later when the movie made its return voyage to Chinese cinemas in 3D.

Among consumers fuelling the trend towards increased censorship are parents concerned about films that aren't always suitable for audiences of all ages, despite being endorsed as such by the government.

ABOVE: Movie-goers watching Titanic 3D, Taiyuan, Shanxi province, 2012

When Zhang Yimou's epic The Flowers of War was released in 2011, much of its violence and scenes of sexual assault were kept in to highlight atrocities committed by Japanese soldiers during the Nanjing Massacre in World War II; one scene, in which a bound woman is raped and stabbed by a soldier, was a common cue for parents to escort crying children from cinemas.

Wu, who has lobbied for a film ratings system in China since 1995, said classifying movies should be "mandatory for society and the film industry".

"As a cinema operator, I constantly get complaints from angry audiences about why kids are allowed to see certain movies. We get a lot of complaints from parents for not telling them in advance if a movie isn't suitable for kids, some who even ask for refunds. But we can't stop parents from taking their children to see certain movies," said Wu.

Credit: Reuters

Momentum to bring in a film ratings system grew in 2004, when the government sought public consultation to draft the country's first film law. Despite generating fanfare from state media, the bill that would have paved the way for a ratings system was rejected by lawmakers the following year.

Cinema lobbyists who are also members of the Chinese People's Political Consultative Conference (CPPCC), a political advisory body that convenes each year, have abandoned their calls for a ratings system at the behest of leaders, said Wu.

"Officials knock on every [cinema representatives'] door and say: 'Do not submit any proposal for a ratings system.' I know some of the members are prepared, like [directors] Zhang Yimou and Feng Xiaogang, to submit this proposal, but officials tell them not to," he added.

As the sole licensed importer of revenue-sharing films, the state-owned China Film →

→ Group has bottleneck control over which international films make it into the country. Each year, 35 foreign movies are allowed to be imported and return up to 25 per cent of gross ticket sales to copyright holders.

However, Hollywood's quest to cash in on the Chinese market has meant conceding to "suggested edits" proposed by the State Administration of Press, Publication, Radio, Film and Television (SAPPRFT), China's cross-media watchdog created when SARFT and the General Administration of Press and Publication merged in April 2013.

When Cloud Atlas hit Chinese cinemas in January 2011, the sci-fi epic was cut by 40 minutes. Skyfall, released by the China Film Group the same month as part of its tactic to limit foreign films' box office takings, suffered a similar fate, with scenes that featured a Chinese character being killed by a French hit man scrubbed.

Bowing to censors is necessary for overseas filmmakers to clinch a coveted spot at Chinese cinemas

Jonathan Landreth, a veteran media and entertainment journalist who opened the Hollywood Reporter's Beijing bureau, said bowing to censors is necessary for overseas filmmakers to clinch a coveted spot at Chinese cinemas.

"There's no sign that the studios really care [about movies being censored]. Frankly, directors seem to be caving as well. No director has stood up and said, 'Forget it. We're going to turn our backs on this for artistic integrity,'" he said.

"The result of having no ratings system is that it is at the whim of the censors to decide what goes into the theatres. Censors can hide behind the lack of a ratings system to block any film."

Despite having influential friends in the government and the clout of being from a showbiz family, Wu has still been left frustrated by officials, which he describes as the "least liked among all watchdogs".

"The current government wants to have more control. Over the past decade, China has politically gone backwards. Censors should be educated. The door to the country is open and cannot be closed," said Wu, the nephew of 1930s silent film actress Hu Die, better known in China as "Madame Butterfly".

During the film development stage of Wu's 2006 domestic thriller Curiosity Kills the Cat, he received a phone call from the head of the Beijing Film Development Lab, who said reels containing sex scenes would be burned.

"I went to the lab to talk to the general manager, who told me that they must destroy the scenes; otherwise, the film bureau would punish them," Wu recalled.

Wu explained the standoff over the phone to the film bureau's deputy chief, who ordered the lab's general manager to stand down. In another brush with controversy, promotion of the movie was pulled at the last minute on China Central Television's movie channel, CCTV-6, in what Wu alleges was a ploy from the producers of Curse of the Golden Flower, a big budget drama that edged out Wu's film as China's entry for Best Foreign Language Film at the 2006 Academy Awards.

After a round of heated late-night phone calls between Wu and the film bureau, CCTV-6 relented and aired the promotion.

"A lot of young directors have no such power or guts to do this kind of thing," Wu laughed. "The biggest problem is the lack of transparency. You can see how many movies have been ruined because of this process. Graduates at film academies are like caged birds. For this generation [of filmmakers], I don't think they can make great movies."

Officials from SAPPRFT did not reply to Index's interview requests.

In China's soft-power offensive, cinema has been one of cultural pillars, even if

ABOVE: Bilingual Chinese and English movie posters at a multiplex in China

Credit: Joe Fox/Radharc Images/Alamy

cracking the overseas market has meant relying on martial arts-dominated epics, such as Hero (2002) and House of the Flying Daggers (2004), along with Sino-US collaborations of more recent years, which include The Karate Kid (2010) and Man of Tai Chi (2013).

In an effort to speed up its quest for cinema's holy grail, an Academy Award, the government took the rare move in July 2013 of loosening some controls on filmmakers by no longer requiring screenplays to be approved before filming begins.

Robert Cain, a producer and entertainment industry consultant who has been doing business in China since 1987, said having screenplays reviewed by censors is a "scary prospect" for Hollywood, which has led some filmmakers to think twice about what goes into their screenplays.

"As movie production companies become more aware of China, there has been a degree of self-censorship," said Cain, a production executive on the 2008 Academy Award-nominated film Mongol, which was partially shot in China.

"As long as there's a single party concerned about controlling messages received in the media, it's hard to see the government ceding that control to others. What weighs on the side of having less censorship is that China has had a really hard time distributing its films, TV programmes and, ultimately, its culture abroad."

Even though few Chinese directors and screenwriters have the celebrity of their American rivals, Landreth said this doesn't reflect a lack of skilled home-grown filmmakers.

"There are plenty of talented writers in China. However, many of them have grown up in a system where they are always looking over their shoulder. They know that if they write without fear or favour they might not get distributed, hence they can't make a living out of it. It is about self-censorship."

A common argument not to adopt a film ratings system is that it presents a slippery slope; censors often quash calls to classify films by claiming it would result in a surge of gratuitous pornography and violence.

"It seems somebody higher up, way above the censorship board or the film regulating agency, has determined that the adoption of a ratings system is tantamount to permitting →

→ all immoral things to be depicted on screen and, ultimately, the degradation of Chinese society," said Raymond Zhou, well-known film critic and the author of A Practical Guide to Chinese Cinema 2002-2012. "This mentality is similar to the era before China opened the stock market, when some people deemed it as the surest sign of capitalism and hence the fall of socialism."

Zhou, also a columnist at the state-run China Daily, describes censorship as one of "three forces", along with piracy and domestic filmmakers' lack of familiarity with genre conventions, that threaten to stifle the creativity of Chinese directors and screenwriters.

But he also points out the benefits of the current system, saying it encourages domestic filmmakers to push the boundaries of censorship.

"It forces a filmmaker to think of ingenious ways for expression, which is sometimes more artistically interesting than a direct statement. For example, no homosexual content is allowed under the current system, yet there are many movies with obvious gay characters or heavily gay content," he said. Wayne Wang's 2011 historical drama Snow Flower and the Secret Fan is a case in point, Zhou said, highlighting a relationship between two female characters that draws on "lesbian customs popular in some parts of China in the old days".

"You may say it is a form of hypocrisy, but hinting at something is a more sophisticated form of artistic expression and also conforms to Chinese tradition and aesthetics. Of course, if you want to be China's Quentin Tarantino, you'll be doomed." X

Tom Fearon is a journalist for China Central Television CCTV and the Global Times. Before working in China, he was a regular contributor to The Phnom Penh Post

Not over and not out

43(1): 153/155 | DOI: 10.1177/0306422014522571

Tel Aviv is known as one of the world's top gay travel destinations. But, asks **Daniella Peled,** are Israeli politicians exploiting the city's liberal image to mask the anti-gay rhetoric?

STROLLING THROUGH THE balmy streets of Tel Aviv, it would be easy to believe you had arrived in the promised land for gays and lesbians. Same-sex couples hold hands at the bijoux coffee stalls along leafy Rothschild Boulevard, and on Hilton beach, men with chiseled abs play *matkot*, a unique ball game beloved by Israelis.

Nearby is Independence Park, once upon a time the city's first cruising hotspot. Rainbow pride flags flutter on numerous verandas and there is very little, if any, homophobic harassment in the city, which has long had openly gay city councillors and an annual raucous pride parade. Tel Aviv is out, proud and regularly voted as one of the world's top gay travel destinations.

Whether this utopia really represents Israeli society outside what many citizens derisorily call "the Tel Aviv bubble" is less clear.

Israel's image as a gay haven is often used as a political tool not only in the domestic sphere, but far more frequently and publicly in the service of Israel's international diplomacy.

Zionist lobbyists enthusiastically exploit Tel Aviv's liberal image as a counterpoint to the persecution many gay men and women experience in surrounding Arab countries. What better example demonstrates, they argue, that their country is "a villa in a jungle", as it was famously described by former Prime Minister Ehud Barak? They like to highlight how remarkably enlightened the Israeli Defence Forces are when it comes to gay rights – in 1993, they opened the draft to all, regardless of sexual orientation, and partners of lesbian, gay, bisexual and transgendered (LGBT) career soldiers enjoy now the same benefits as heterosexual spouses.

Others, however, say this is nothing but "pinkwashing" – using LGBT rights to mask the realities of an ongoing, brutal military occupation. In Israel and abroad, some LGBT activists claim their cause is being manipulated for propaganda purposes, arguing that it's impossible to separate gay rights from wider issues of equality. While Israel continues to oppress the Palestinians, the country deserves no credit for its promotion and protection of gay rights.

On the other hand, many assert that Israel deserves credit for the distance it has travelled towards equality and tolerance for gay people. Arthur Slepian, who runs A Wider Bridge, an organisation which aims to build stronger ties between Jewish LGBT communities around the world, feels that the claims of "pinkwashing" are both unfair and unhelpful. "The pinkwashing accusations really devalue the work of Israel's LGBT community, who have worked hard for →

ABOVE: The Israeli draft is open to people of any sexuality

→ the past 25 years or more to secure their rights and to make LGBT people a visible and proud part of Israeli society," he says. He adds that, on the whole, Israel has been an impressive promoter of LGBT rights and equality.

But the real issue is that in Israel, as in many other countries, LGBT rights bring the fault lines between secular liberal values and religious ones into sharp focus. For example, consider another, much smaller, pride festival that is held each year just 45 minutes' drive from Tel Aviv. In Jerusalem, the holy city, those organising the event to celebrate the LGBT community must take significant security precautions, because the festival has in the past been marred by a number of attacks and violent demonstrations. In 2007, the government approved legislation allowing the Jerusalem city hall to prevent further parades from taking place. The legislation was never passed, but the fact that steps were taken to restrict the event illustrates that it is in many ways vulnerable.

"Orthodox Judaism is very hostile to LGBT people and trans people in particular," says Nora Grinberg, a 63-year-old trans advocate and activist. "In Israel, the official and public Judaism is only Orthodox. There are little islands of conservative and reform Judaism but they give way to a brand of Orthodoxy that in recent years is more extreme and retrograde."

This religious hegemony has an impact on the lives of all Israelis, regardless of sexual orientations. For instance, while it's true that gay couples enjoy most of the same rights as straight couples, Israeli law does not permit same-sex marriage or civil partnerships and marriage ceremonies are carried out by the religious establishment.

Homophobic rhetoric from right-wing politicians and religious sectors is as unremarkable as anti-Arab discourse. In a political culture where narrow interest groups are regularly courted, politicians often shamelessly play and pander to their constituents, and this can include responding positively to homophobic views expressed by some of them.

In November 2013, Moshe Abutbul, the newly re-elected mayor of the mostly Orthodox town of Beit Shemesh and a member of the ultra-Orthodox Shas party said: "We have none of those things [gays] here. Thank God, this city is holy and pure."

Abutbul hardly improved matters when he backtracked, saying that he was not aware there were gays in his town and that he had been talking about paedophiles anyway.

Israel's Palestinian community is often deeply traditional, leading to some hostility towards LGBT people and issues associated with them. Also among the large Russian-speaking community there are those who

Credit: Yannis Behrakis/Reuters

mirror the anti-gay tendencies of the Putin government back in Moscow.

"Most homosexuals are people who experienced sexual abuse at a very young age," Anastassia Michaeli, a Russian-born former parliamentarian from the right-wing Israel is Our Home party (Yisrael Beitenu), which is associated with, and widely supported by, immigrants from the former Soviet Union, told the Knesset in June 2012. "They are miserable, these homosexuals... Eventually they commit suicide at the age of 40."

The most recent government, formed by Prime Minister Binyamin Netanyahu earlier this year, is a rare thing in Israeli politics – a coalition that does not include any of the country's ultra-Orthodox parties. It does,

LGBT rights bring the fault lines between secular liberal values and religious ones into sharp focus

however, include the Jewish Home party (Habayit Hayedhdi), an extreme right-wing religious party that champions settlements in the West Bank while also trying to cultivate a certain aura of liberalism in order to attract secular voters.

The party has not been keen about openly addressing LGBT issues, but in recent weeks it has strenuously opposed a series of legislative amendments, along with members of the Israel is Our Home party (Yisrael Beiteinu), that would have granted same-sex parents equality on tax and mortgage benefits. They argued that these amendments, put forward by the more centrist parties in the coalition, were an attempt to introduce same-sex marriage by stealth.

The economics minister and leader of the Jewish Home party, Naftali Bennet – who, as the right-wing's main standard-bearer in Israel's parliament, recently called the Palestinians "a thorn in our backside" – explained his party's opposition to the amendments, and subconsciously perhaps, articulated the conflicting attitudes to gay rights within Israeli society.

"These are two clashing values," he said. "I am for 'live and let live', but this clashes with the values of Israel as a Jewish state."

Bennet views both LGBT equality and Palestinian independence as intolerable. Not all Israelis agree, but the state has yet to define just what these values are, and what they mean for its conflicts, both internal and external.

Daniella Peled is editor at the Institute for War and Peace Reporting, and has reported widely from across the Middle East

Indian magnates fight an uphill battle to control the media

43(1): 156/158 | DOI: 10.1177/0306422014522581

Wealthy Indian families have been trying to shape the news in their interests since independence. Journalist **Prayaag Akbar** asks if, with increased scrutiny from websites and social media, they can really stop news they don't like being published

ECONOMIC EXPANSION OVER the last two decades has meant that the power-distribution within India's business class is no longer oligarchic, but the great wealth amassed by some magnates – the term favoured locally is "industrialist" – means it retains distinctly oligarchic characteristics. One of the expressions of this concentration of economic power is the desire among some of the richest of these industrialists to control the narrative around the behemoth corporations they run, whether through direct ownership of the media or the exercise of influence in other ways.

An example of this phenomenon was revealed in 2010, when the transcripts of a series of taped conversations between the publicist Niira Radia, who had links to two of the biggest of the country's corporations, Tata Sons and Reliance Industries, and a number of very influential politicians and journalists, were published by two news weeklies. The transcripts, known as the "Radia tapes", revealed a degree of collusion and information-sharing between these three vital nodes of society that left many in India greatly disturbed, but perhaps not surprised. Such influence-mongering is seen by most as common practice.

The real surprise was that the transcripts had been published at all. It is well known now that other media houses had been given the transcripts but had chosen not to publish them before the first magazine, Open, a relatively small publication, went ahead, rapidly followed by another current affairs weekly, Outlook. In doing so these weeklies seem to have disturbed a venerable compact between business journalists and large corporations in India that had long resulted in a failure to examine fully the practices of such companies. It is sometimes argued that it was the same compact that, in the decades following independence from colonial rule, cemented the quaint but widely accepted notion of the Indian industrialist as benevolent patriarch instead of profit-seeker.

One of the interesting developments in the short time since the publication of those transcripts has been the entry of some of India's biggest corporate houses into the media business, though it should be pointed out that there is no reason to believe the two are related. This development has been especially noticeable in television news. In the past few years three of India's richest men, all previously without any direct news media interests, acquired significant ownership stakes in the biggest media groups in the country. These companies had grown at unsustainable rates in the years of India's brief economic upswing. During the lean years following the global recession, each struggled for long periods, cutting costs and jobs periodically while searching for an infusion of funds that could revitalise their business.

On the face of it, the new interest of corporate magnates in television companies should have grave implications. Yet there is reason for hope. The problem in India is not one of direct censorship from corporate owners. Interviews and conversations with a number of high-ranking editors and reporters contacted during the writing of this piece indicate something quite different.

The prevailing sentiment is that in this regard it is self-censorship that comes into play. A new owner does not need to send any messages to his journalists, and nor will he risk his reputation by doing anything so unseemly. Yet there is no denying that the importance of keeping these individuals happy motivates editorial boards to act differently than they would otherwise. In the same vein, as in the case of the Radia tapes, editors who did not carry the story also did so out of professional fealty, unwilling to impugn the high-ranking journalists involved.

How does one address this self-censorship? As the media base in India broadens, and bearing in mind the unique challenges to information-control that the web and social media present, perhaps there is no need to. Here is a counter-intuitive example: in May last year, India's sixth-richest man, Kumar Mangalan Birla, acquired a large stake in

ABOVE: A woman reads India Today magazine, owned by Living Media. India's sixth-richest man, Kumar Mangalan Birla, acquired a 27.5 per cent stake in the company in 2012

Credit: dbimages/Alamy

Living Media Group, which runs a popular news channel and India's biggest news weekly. In October, he was named in a preliminary report filed by India's Central Bureau of Intelligence in a matter pertaining to the allocation of coal deposits to one of his companies.

The news channel he partly owns and the daily newspaper owned and operated by his sister largely ignored the news. Yet every other major newspaper led with it on the front page and every other news channel reported on it frequently.

India now has a media space large enough to ensure that a story like this will comprehensively enter the public domain. Crucially, the social media sphere has been especially diligent in taking news channels and newspapers to task for what they see as →

→ biased reporting. There is in-depth analyses on websites about who reports on what. It takes its toll on reputations.

The under-reporting of the Birla case by the media organs he and his family own has been seen as a derogation of media responsibilities, and certainly a disservice to their consumers. However, Indian media has been funded by rich corporate families since independence. When it is not censoring itself, it

In the past few years three of India's richest men have acquired significant ownership stakes in the biggest media groups in the country

has operated with a great deal of freedom. For instance, the publications that first published the Radia tapes are both owned by industrialist families, but the decision to publish was taken at an editorial level. As the public avails itself of more and more disparate sources of news, the ability of the rich and politically powerful to control what is written and said about them seems to diminish by the month. ☒

Prayaag Akbar is associate editor of the Sunday Guardian, an Indian weekly newspaper

ABOVE: A record store in Norwich stands defiant against the digital age

Credit: T.M.O. Buildings/Alamy

In this section

Bittersweet symphony

43(1): 162/165 | DOI: 10.1177/0306422013520276

Has technology helped or hindered musicians' artistic expression? Journalist and musician **Ed Wallis** reports

THERE IS A familiar debate about whether the onset of the digital age has killed the music industry's business model or whether it has led to a democratic revolution. The answer, as ever, lies somewhere in between.

Various established artists have bemoaned the impact of illegal filesharing on record sales. Fleetwood Mac's Stevie Nicks has claimed "the internet has destroyed rock…I'm financially stable. I'm okay. But what about the kids trying to make it in this business?" Blondie's Debbie Harry agrees: "Computers and the internet and downloading songs completely ruined the music industry and everything artists used to work for." But Greg Kot, author of How the Internet Changed Music, suggests that assessing the internet's influence is more complicated and multi-faceted than that. "The biggest problem a band has is getting its music heard. For years, the music industry was confined to four multinational corporations that dominated the revenue stream of 70 per cent of the music coming in, and four or five radio conglomerates that controlled what music was going out. Now all that has been broken up into millions and millions of little pieces and subcultures and niches that are serving small, really dedicated communities of music lovers."

Overall, despite the changes wrought by the digital era, the music industry's performance is reasonably robust, worth £3.5bn ($5.7bn) to the UK economy according to recent research by UK Music. However, there is a structural change that people should probably be more worried about than they are. Illegal filesharing is having an impact on the shape of our culture, as well as on opportunities to participate in it.

The truth is, at the top, despite ongoing concern at falling record sales, the guys with the gold-plated cell phones are still managing to do okay. Forbes magazine recently published a list of the highest earning musicians of the year, headed by Madonna, with $125m and a top 20 worth well over a collective annual billion, mostly based on the continuing rude health of live music. While revenue from recorded music sales has dropped dramatically, when taking into account concert, publishing and other streams, total revenues of the music industry have actually increased, from around $50bn in 1998 to around $60bn in 2011, according to a study by professional business services firm PricewaterhouseCoopers.

Big acts are able to leverage their star status in a different way than before. Mobile phone company Samsung paid $5m to secure advance rights for Jay-Z's new album for owners of their latest Galaxy phones to access through a free app. Similarly, Madonna cut a 10-year "360" deal with Live Nation, worth a reported $120bn, which allows for the exploitation of all aspects of her brand.

And the new technologies that are supposed to be killing record sales are beginning to turn serious profits for some shareholders (many of whom are the same people that run the major record companies). Spotify has a market capitalisation estimated at over $4bn and is waiting to float, and although it is still a loss-making enterprise, the nature of tech funding means it has netted its founder Daniel Ek £190 million ($309.6 million) and put him 10th in the Sunday Times Music Millionaires Rich List, equal with Mick Jagger.

Lower down the food chain, the possibilities of digital technology have made it much easier to record and disseminate music. Some recent music trends reflect this: the prominent feature of 2012's "chillwave" was the sound of people in their bedrooms singing softly into computer reverb plug-ins. People can easily make songs on recording software like GarageBand and use tools like Tunecore to sell them online. Some of these acts will go overground and become wider success stories; some will remain personal concerns with niche audiences. But the tools are there if you just want to make some music, put it out there and see what happens.

ABOVE: Independent record shops participate in Record Stor Day, conceived in 2007, Soho, London

Credit: Matthew Chattle/Alamy

Where there is a growing structural imbalance is among a "squeezed middle": the collapse of record sales has hit a broad swathe of struggling working bands. The rewards of the music industry are increasingly congregating around the top and new opportunities are, perhaps, offering most to those at the bottom.

The point was made most clearly by Andrew Falkous, singer for Future of the Left, in a blog about the leaking of their second album. "Please be careful, or we'll get the world we deserve. Hobby bands who can tour once every few years if they're lucky, and the superstars...running the corporate sponsored marathon of £80-a-ticket arena tours and television adverts 'til their loveless hearts explode." This was written in 2009 and reprinted in full by UK Music as part of its anti-filesharing campaign. All the evidence suggests Falkous's dystopia is creeping into existence. The majority of music acts are unable to leverage the sponsorship deals, command the huge ticket prices or secure the big-paying publishing syncs that allow the lucky few to continue to thrive. Continually declining record sales – US album sales are at a historic low according to Nielsen SoundScan – are still the bread and butter of many working artists. As Nigel Godrich, Radiohead's long-term producer, noted on his blog, the new high revenues "are being generated solely by larger already established artists who can set very high prices for →

→ their tickets and T-shirts to make up for their lost other revenue. Smaller artists who are not in the position to charge anything like the Rolling Stones or Madonna are not the ones to benefit from these new incomes."

The situation is not being helped, some argue, by streaming services such as Spotify or Pandora. The music industry has invested heavily in legal streaming in the war against illegal downloading, but the low returns to artists generate controversy. On the music website Pitchfork, Damon Krukowski wrote that his band Galaxie 500's song Tugboat "was played 7,800 times on Pandora, for which its three songwriters were paid a collective total of 21 cents, or seven cents each.

As Thom Yorke put it in a tweet: "Make no mistake new artists you discover on #Spotify will not get paid. Meanwhile shareholders will shortly be rolling in it. Simples."

Spotify pays better: for the 5,960 times Tugboat was played there, Galaxie 500's songwriters went collectively into triple digits: $1.05 (35 cents each)." As Thom Yorke put it in a tweet: "Make no mistake new artists you discover on #Spotify will not get paid. meanwhile shareholders will shortly be rolling in it. Simples."

It seems little coincidence that these changes in the financial structure of the music industry are taking place at the same time as a noticeable social restructuring. John Major recently criticised a "collapse in social mobility", saying that "in every single sphere of British influence, the upper echelons of power in 2013 are held overwhelmingly by the privately educated or the affluent middle class". Journalist John Harris pointed out in The Guardian: "People who have had expensive educations dominate journalism, law, finance – and, of late, even the supposedly meritocratic powerhouse that is British pop music (witness Mumford and Sons, Florence Welch, Lily Allen, Laura Marling et al)." Word magazine found that the majority of artists from an October 2010 chart week had been privately educated, compared to the same week in 1990, when nearly 80 per cent were educated at state school.

The long-term social stranglehold of the middle classes has been strengthened recently by the rise of the unpaid internship. For many of the kudos-carrying careers in public life, a period spent working for free is now a requirement. Ross Perlin wrote in Intern Nation, his expose of the proliferation of unpaid work in the modern economy, "those who can't afford to work without pay are effectively shut out...Internships quietly embody and promote inequalities of opportunity." In the past it has been record companies who have supported fledgling acts through the payment of advances on future record sales. With record sales on the wrong side of the rebalancing of the record industry, those funds are harder to come by, advantaging those with some pre-existing financial capital to support the early stages of their careers.

Not only does this trend seem to be creating duller music, there is a fairness issue at its heart that needs to be acknowledged. There is also a liberty question, but it's probably not one of freedom of expression. You can say what you want – but will you get the chance to say it? The issue at stake, returning to Isaiah Berlin, is one of positive rather than negative liberty. No one is really being prevented from expressing themselves, but are they being enabled? And is that ability being equally shared?

One positive step would be to implement the recommendations of the Hargreaves Report, which was commissioned by the UK coalition government, to modernise copyright laws for the digital age. The report's findings managed the remarkable feat of uniting musicians' unions, the music industry and open rights campaigners, who all supported it. But two years after it was published, it is still sitting on a shelf somewhere in the depths of Whitehall, the government having blinked in the face of opposition from content providers. A similar timidity has been seen over the implementation of the Digital Economy Act, where action on copyright infringement has been delayed by legal challenges from internet providers.

The music industry also has a responsibility to ensure it doesn't become a closed shop. It was much criticised for its lateness in waking up to the threat posed by illegal downloading, and then its reliance on ineffective legalistic responses. But if streaming is the answer – and it remains to be seen if it is – it should take seriously the concerns of artists and labels at the low royalty rate, and investigate proposals for splitting access to streamed music, with cheap access to established acts' back catalogues and a higher price for new music.

It isn't all doom and gloom in the music industry. Independent retailer Rough Trade understood that people were prepared to pay for experiences you couldn't get on the internet, like knowledgeable staff and a model of the record shop as a cultural hub, and recently expanded, opening a new store in Brooklyn. Digital music sales overtook physical for the first time in 2012; vinyl sales are up and at the annual Record Store Day and Independent Label Market show certain niche markets are able to thrive. The industry needs to use these positive trends as a platform to keep finding ways to go with the grain of technological change and allowing freedom of expression, while at the same time protecting revenues and supporting new artists. One good initiative is the Momentum Music Fund, supported by the Arts Council and Performing Rights Society, which provides development grants of up to £15k ($24,600) to artists.

With politicians of all parties struggling to answer the economic challenges posed by the global financial crash of 2008, the creative industries offer the UK a clear competitive advantage in a globalised market place and an opportunity to create a patriotic and productive high-skill economy. We need to create the right economic and legal framework to ensure opportunities to participate in a thriving and innovative industry are available to all.

Ed Wallis is a musician and editor of the Fabian Review. He has a new record out this month

METAL FINISHING HANDBOOK
Digital Fundamentals

The busier booksellers of Burma

43(1): 166/169 | DOI: 10.1177/0306422014522577

Until August 2012 every publication in Burma (including newspapers, books, and cartoons) needed to be approved in advance by the Press Scrutiny and Registration Division of Burma's Ministry of Information. The lifting of the 1962 Printers and Publishers Registration Act marked an important step in the country's transition. The accompanying editorial in the Myanmar Times underlined its significance noting "the removal of pre-publication censorship is another load of cement being poured into the foundations of democracy here in Myanmar". A photo essay by **Cedric Arnold** and words by **Mary O'Shea**

LEFT: U Hla Min Aung, owner of New Vision bookshop on Street 37th in Downtown Rangoon stands amongst floor-to-ceiling stacks of books. At the entrance door, books by opposition leader Aung San Suu Kyi and her independence hero father are proudly on display. Less than two years ago, this would have been unthinkable.

THE BIRDS
စာအုပ်ရောင်းဝယ်ရေ

ABOVE: Early morning, workers at a Yangon bookshop take stock of their inventory. At the front of the shop, the now commonplace poster of Aung San Suu Kyi that one finds all over the city, could have caused the business to close just a few years ago. The Burmese are avid readers, bring books and newspapers on every trip be it on the Rangoon river ferry, busses, trains and the reading will often start heated discussions at teashops.

LEFT BELOW: U Hla Min Aung's daughter eats her lunch amidst more piles of books that invade every room including the kitchen at New Vision; everything from rare British colonial era tomes to traditional Burmese fairytales. In celebration of the country's new literary freedom, the first ever international literary festival was held in Burma in 2013, featuring a host of internationally acclaimed writers, such as Timothy Garton Ash, Vikram Seth, Jung Chang, William Dalrymple and Fergal Keane, as well as almost 60 local literary figures. Presided over by patron Aung San Suu Kyi, the Irrawaddy Literary Festival was the brainchild of Jane Heyn, the wife of the British Ambassador to Burma. The idea of having a literary festival first came to her when touring old bookshops in Rangoon. She was struck by how "Burmese bookshops were managing to create books out of nothing". How they would photocopy precious uncensored literary editions and make "one text go a million miles". The 2014 Irrawaddy Literary Festival took place in Mandalay on the grounds of the Kuthodaw Pagoda, said to be home to the "world's largest book".

LEFT ABOVE: Impromptu book bazaars are a prominent feature of the downtown Yangon landscape, with piles of books spread out across pavements on tarpaulin mats or lined up on makeshift street-side shelves, hastily constructed each morning. Some of these street bookshops also act as teashops.

43.01

CULTURE

Slowly opening door

43(1): 170/172 | DOI: 10.1177/0306422014522938

Across all art forms artists, comedians, film-makers, writers, translators and publishers have been very quick off the mark to make the most of the loosening of censorship regulations and increase in access to the arts and publications across Burma, says **Julia Farrington**

A FEW YEARS ago vendors would not dream of selling Aung San Suu Kyi memorabilia or activists of giving out political campaigning literature for the opposition party in the streets. These days walking along those same streets you would find many stalls and books selling t-shirts, keyrings, mugs and even pendants all with her image on them as well as political campaigning paraphernalia.

Visiting a guesthouse in early 2012, I returned to my room with Aung San Suu Kyi trinkets to be told by the owner that a year earlier even asking where Aung San Suu Kyi's lived would have forced him to tell the authorities and probabably have me followed.

Since 2010 when Aung San Suu Kyi was released, as detailed in Index's recent Burma: Freedom of Expression in Transition report, censorship boards have been abolished, the leading opposition political party the NLD has been allowed to regroup and by-elections have given leading National League for Democracy figures seats in parliament for the first time. While the political situation remains volatile, the art world has changed considerably. There are now international film festivals, and there's been some reform of media laws. While these are not perfect they have changed how reporting happens.

Dr Thant Thaw Kaung, executive director of the book publisher and distributor, Myanmar Book Centre said: "Now is a really good time to read so many news books on... politics, history, fiction and non-fiction which were previously banned. Books on politics are in the highest demand....biographies, memoirs of political prisoners become best sellers nowadays."

But not everyone is so positive. Blogger, writer, and former political prisoner Nay Phone Latt, in a recent interview with International PEN, conceded that the situation for writers in Burma had "changed a little bit". The new censorship laws are seen by many as little more than a switch of tactics, the laws now penalising work that has already been published rather than at the pre-publication stage. Political interference isn't the only problem facing publishers. According to an International Publishers' Association report "deep-rooted infrastructural and training problems create significant challenges... These problems are linked to the decades of economic decline the country has faced under military rule".

So even though every street vendor and bookshop gives the Aung San Suu Kyi section pride of place in their displays, it is not going to be plain sailing for publishers.

THE MYANMAR TIMES
Myanmar's first international weekly
August 27 - September 2, 2012
Volume 33, No. 641 1200 Kyats
Pic: Boothee
MYANMAR TIMES
Goodbye to the red pen
But what does the future hold for Myanmar's print media? Read the full coverage on **pages 3, 4 and 5**
free press set to conti

ABOVE: The front page of the Myanmar Times (27th August 2012) marking the lifting of censorship laws

Credit: Cedric Arnold

Burma remains an extremely poor country and the majority of people work extremely long hours; the average family will spend 68 per cent of the household budget on food. Even with literacy at 92.7 per cent (according to UNESCO), making the country one of the most literate in the world, reading is regarded by many as a luxury. Nay Phone Latt said "there isn't a strong readership in Burma and despite a population of 60 million, the circulation of any book usually only runs to 1,000. So it's just not profitable to write".

Waing Waing, joint secretary of the Myanmar Publishers and Booksellers Association, said: "Many publishers including myself publish new titles and the market varies... Apart from the dramatic increase in the demands for political books, the whole market remains quite the same as before. The market accepts some [new titles] but many can't penetrate the market." Lucas Stewart, literary advisor at the British Council said: "Most of the publishers I meet are not that positive about the current state of publishing". One publisher had told him →

→ he was only able to continue because he subsidises his publishing company with his successful monk clothing business. However James Byrne, editor of Bones Will Crow, a bilingual book of Burmese poetry, says that Monument Books in Yangon, a very stylish modern bookshop, "is selling books like chocolate".

Publishers in Burma are not exempt from the influence of the internet, even though penetration is currently estimated at between 1 and 7 per cent. A recent article in the business pages of The New York Times, paints a bleak picture for print media. "Despite expectations of pent-up demand, publishers

The circulation of any book usually only runs to 1,000. So it's just not profitable to write

say they are suffering from a lack of advertising and competition from the internet." Following the governments granting licences to publish Burmese daily newspapers for the first time in 60 years, 12 new independent dailies starting in April this year, three of which have already folded.

Lucas Stewart, who runs a project promoting writers in ethnic minority languages called Hidden Worlds, for the British Council, said that writers from this group are currently rarely published. This is another legacy of military dictatorship, where until recently teaching ethnic literature in schools had been banned. Stewart told Index that "ethnic regions lack the printing facilities to press their own works and publishers in Yangon and Mandalay don't publish works in ethnic minority languages claiming there is no market for it".

The new Myanmar PEN Centre, currently based in Yangon and launched late last year, is also addressing this deeply entrenched imbalance by encouraging membership amongst ethnic minority writers and aims to publish a multi-lingual anthology of new writing at the end of the first year.

PEN Myanmar came about thanks to a 15-year campaign led by writer and former political prisoner, Ma Thida. It is part of a critical shift to a democratic society, where civil society organisations have increasing influence. Like all PEN centres around the world, it is a writers club and since it was launched last year is attracting a large volume of applications for membership. However, as Paul Finnegan, centres and committees officer of PEN International said, not all these applicants will be successful. "The independence of its membership is absolutely crucial and PEN Myanmar are trying to admit only suitable young writers who are not affiliated with other writers' associations, such as the National Writers Association, which are often seen as overly influenced by the government. Board members of the centre are formally required to give up their membership of any other writers association in order to help retain this independence". Nay Phone Latt, a newly elected board member of Myanmar PEN, speaks for the many people who are working to make Myanmar a more just society when he says; "The future of our country is in the hands of its citizens. How much we can try our best will determine the destiny of our country." X

Julia Farrington travelled to Burma for Index in February 2012, and again in March 2013 as part of a programme of professional development for contemporary artists in Yangon and Mandalay

Rebel noise

43(1): 173/180 | DOI: 10.1177/0306422014525112

When the Turkish government mistook her play for a dress rehearsal for real-life events in Gezi Park, playwright **Meltem Arikan**, now forced into exile, found herself on the frontline of her country's battles over politics, civil society and artistic freedom. Here, Index publishes an extract from her award-winning play for the first time in English

WHEN PLAYWRIGHT AND author Meltem Arikan began writing her play Mi Minor, it was an attempt to capture the lives of ordinary people today as the relationship between citizens and the government rapidly changes. Across protest movements in the Middle East, North Africa and Europe, social media is helping to transform how people communicate about politics and culture, and this is one of the play's themes.

During the summer of 2013, when the protests over Gezi Park were being broadcast and reported around the world, some of Turkey's most powerful pro-government media found the new media challenging. Despite extensive research to ensure Mi Minor was truly international, Arikan was accused of using the play to stir up protests. Politicians attacked Arikan on social media and television, while members of the public were encouraged to join the campaign against her. She received a number of rape and death threats. She fled Turkey, fearing for her life, and is currently living in the United Kingdom.

She told Index in a recent interview: "After I got involved in social media I didn't care about individual countries any more because I came to realize that interactions on social media happen regardless of the borders of distances, languages, nations, religions or ideologies. This inspired me to create a play."

→ The play is set in the fictional country of Pinima, where the president starts by banning the musical note Mi. It features a character called the Pianist, who defies the musical ban, and goes on to report on events in the country via Twitter. By doing this, he launches a role-playing game with the audience, who then choose to take part and support a game set out by the president or to side with the rebellious Pianist.

SCENE 1

Before the play starts the Pianist sends a tweet: "I will be playing Chopin at the square. Please come or else watch me on Ustream." She provides information about her emotional state plus the audience's emotional state from her point of view.

CHIEF What are you doing here?

PIANIST I'm playing piano.

CHIEF No...! Apparently you're playing Chopin.

PIANIST Yes. I'm playing Chopin's 44th Mazurka.

CHIEF As a woman, are you not ashamed to play men that you don't know?

Digital Actor#1, in English, summarises what's happening to the Pianist on the Ustream URL, and then sends a tweet.

PIANIST Chopin is one of the most famous composers in the world.

CHIEF Lying to the eyes of the government...

PIANIST Lying?

CHIEF How much older am I than you?

PIANIST I have no idea.

ABOVE: Meltem Arikan

CHIEF Of course you have no idea. That's what women are like...I'm at least 20 years older than you. If he were that famous I'd have known about him before you. I don't know him so....

CHIEF (*Asks the policeman*) Do you know the man?

POLICEMAN No chief. I don't know any famous person at all.

CHIEF Did you hear that? He doesn't know him too...could there be any celebrity the great government don't know about?

POLICEMAN There can't be, chief.

CHIEF This man is not famous at all. You say he is very famous? Ha? You confuse people's minds and slyly poison our pure society with those noises. That man's music is none of your business.

The policeman walks in front of the piano and pushes the Pianist aside. He pulls police tape around the right side of the piano. And →

→ *then he hangs a piece of paper that says "banned for use" onto the tape.*

PIANIST What are you doing?

CHIEF From now on, that side of the piano is banned for use. You can only play this side. I would ban all of it but you should be thankful to the President. Despite everything, he is very merciful. Your place should be behind bars, anyway...dear girl, is it your business to play a foreign man...and in the middle of the street?

If you are a moral citizen, your telephone being listened to won't disturb you. But if this disturbs you, it proves that you do secret and hidden things, which simply proves that your telephone must be listened to at all times

PIANIST What are you talking about?

CHIEF Don't stare at me like that...whatever the President says goes. Are you questioning the decisions of the magnificent President? My President, he also gave orders to the manufacturers. From now on, all pianos will be shortened. They made this enormous instrument to make ting ting ting sounds. What a pity... its paint, nails, metals...these are all the national wealth of our government, national I say...also, from today, the playing of these men is also banned. Boy, move this away from here.

PIANIST Bach, Mozart, Liszt, Beethoven, Chopin...

The Ustream goes off. The Pianist sends a tweet: "I can't believe this. Treble sounds, pianos and playing Bach, Mozart, Chopin is forbidden."

ABOVE: Turkish protesters, Taksim Square, July 2013. Though some media outlets claimed Mi Minor was a blueprint for protests against Gezi Park, playwright Meltem Arikan says the play is international in its focus

Credit: Georgi Licovski/EPA

SCENE 4

The Pianist and the musicians return to their platform. The digital dialogues continue.

ANCHORMAN Good day and welcome. We'd like to share with you the highly important declaration that was given from the Presidential residence today. According to the declaration, our President hasn't slept for 48 hours and he listened to the telephones of people whom he had randomly chosen. The President declared that this shall be done by him once a week. In his declaration, he underlined that in every country, the telephones are being listened to; however, →

→ they do it behind closed doors. It's never announced to the public whose telephones are listened to. Whereas in our country what the President is doing, in the name of democracy and transparency, should be set as an example to the whole world. This method will make it easier to find the citizens who are abducted by the aliens and they will be treated immediately. As usual, we are now connecting to the square to hear the public opinion. Yes, we're with you.

STREET REPORTER Okay, you're with me. Hello, ladies and gentlemen, we are now asking the public what they think about our President's declaration of listening to the telephones himself and making this a routine operation. What do you think about the declaration from the Presidential residence?

The musician comes next to the men and leans towards the microphone.

MUSICIAN There are things called human rights and privacy, but this operation is absolutely against humanity, against democracy.

MAN A Look, you heard that, right? There you go; today the world is like this because of people who think like him. They say human rights, democracy, freedom but they always ask for some things to be kept confidential.

MUSICIAN Excuse me sir, what are you talking about?

MAN A If you are a moral citizen, your telephone being listened to won't disturb you. But if this disturbs you, it proves that you do secret and hidden things, and which simply proves that your telephone must be listened to at all times.

Pianist sends a tweet: "We will Ustream the speech of the president." Digital Actor#1 translates it into English.

PRESIDENT My people, I couldn't wake up this morning because I didn't sleep last night. I didn't sleep because I thought for you, for your happiness, so I made a decision. Having many choices is not freedom. Minds confuse when choices increase. Choices lead to polarisations, polarisations to hostility. Therefore, I have decided that only two parties will participate in the elections. I am the presidential candidate for both parties. Public voice is very important in a democracy, that's why I decided to have two parties. Even though you don't speak, I hear you my people...Furthermore, ballot boxes, computers and officers being used during the elections will all be history. On Election Day, there will be a 500-metre long running race in the stadium between the two parties, and the party who wins the race will come to power. Running means to be resistant while going forward. From now on, the elections will not go to waste; on the contrary, it will be an actual race that you will all participate in with enthusiasm.

SCENE 26

PIANIST I'm guilty! I want to have freedom of thought and freedom of expression by getting away from all the oppressions of ideologies and religions.

I confess. By destroying the imposed thought patterns on me, I strive to think freely.

I'm guilty! I know that running away from realities is running away from pain.

I confess. All kinds of escape are generated by fear, nurtured by cowards. I do not accept being frightened.

I'm guilty! I do not accept any of the imposed restrictions upon me.

I confess. I draw the borders of my freedom myself.

I'm guilty! By questioning the things you had taught me again and again, I'm giving up on socialisation, on my family, on my beliefs. I confess, mother, wife, lover, I refuse all the roles you've imposed upon me.

I'm guilty! I choose to rebel in order to exist. →

→ I confess, I do not find any of your words important.

I'm guilty! While in transition to the digital world order, I believe in the importance of the creation of new organisations. I confess, I strive for women and men to affirm their existence without belonging to any religion or any ethnicity and I strive for a free new world order.

CHIEF *Holds the Pianist's both hands firmly, handcuffs her.*

You have crossed the line now. No one can save you from my hands. Insult to the unity of sacred family in a public space...openly encouraging people to rebel in a public space...

He turns to the crowd gathered there.

There you see what corruption turns you into. Protect your children; otherwise the aliens will make them rebellions like this. Look and draw a lesson from it... ☒

Translated by Pinar Ogun and Karl Mercer

Meltem Arikan is a Turkish playwright, now based in the United Kingdom. Her 2004 novel Stop Hurting My Flesh tackles sexual abuse as a theme, and was banned in Turkey. She tweets @meltemarikan

HEAD TO HEAD

Are womens' voices in film more powerful than 60 years ago?

OPINION

43(1): 181/185 | DOI: 10.1177/0306422014522917

Olivia J Fox

As a 50-something British actress and screenwriter living in Los Angeles, I've seen both the glitter and the grime of Hollywood. My first job when I washed up on the shores of this movie capital eight years ago garnered me my own trailer at Paramount Studios and a Screen Actor's Guild (SAG) card and, although it has not been exactly smooth sailing since, I believe that there are more opportunities for women in film than ever before.

ABOVE: Olivia J Fox

Credit: Mark Boardman, www.mark-boardman.com

In fact, looking at this year's crop of awards season contenders, it would be hard to deny that women in film are in a better position than they have ever been.

Front runners included Blue Jasmine (a female-driven drama starring Cate Blanchett); Gravity (in which Sandra Bullock shared equal billing with George Clooney); August; Osage County (with strong roles for Meryl Streep and Julia Roberts); American Hustle (gritty characters for Amy Adams and Jennifer Lawrence); Saving Mr Banks (Emma Thompson as Mary Poppins creator PL Travers taking on the Disney machine); and Philomena (starring Judi Dench as a mother looking for her stolen child).

Jane Earl

Things just aren't the way they used to be. Just file through your collection of classic films from the 1930s, 40s and 50s to find feisty women characters who stride across the screen and dominate the action. Bette Davis, Katherine Hepburn, Greta Garbo anyone? And when it comes to running a major studio, Mary Pickford helped set up United Artists back in 1919.

ABOVE: Jane Earl

This year began with the news that the highest-earning film around the world in 2013 was Iron Man 3. A superhero movie aimed predominantly at a young male audience where the female lead character Pepper Potts (Gwyneth Paltrow) plays perpetual →

→ second fiddle to a comic book superhero as his assistant/love interest. You could argue that further down the list of the top 10 grossing films of 2013 one finds The Hunger Games: Catching Fire and Gravity, both featuring strong female lead characters. But those are just two titles in a testosterone-fuelled top 10 that includes Fast & Furious 6, Man of Steel, Thor: The Dark World and three animated features.

Moreover, it's great that female directors like Sophia Coppola and Sarah Polley and performances like that of Emanuelle Riva in Amour are helping to push female voices to the forefront, but the sad truth is that any film that isn't a massive blockbuster like Gravity will only be available on a limited amount of screens. Which means there will be millions who won't get to even see this work unless they live in major metropolitan areas. Even Woody Allen's Blue Jasmine with Cate Blanchett in a leading role received a limited release in Los Angeles and New York and may only get a wider release following Blanchett's Oscar nomination and recent Golden Globe win for Best Actress.

OJF

As a young girl growing up in the 1960s, my screen heroines were somewhat more disparate: tomboys like those personified by Hayley Mills in films such as Pollyanna and The Parent Trap or the impossible glamour of a Bond girl and nothing much in between. Things have moved on apace since then, with far more varied and complex female characters being represented in film and with women as the protagonists of more films than ever before.

Screen heroines have become feistier role models for a new generation: witness Jennifer Lawrence as Katniss in The Hunger Games and Catching Fire, and Rooney Mara and Noomi Rapace as Lisbeth Salander in the US and original Swedish versions of The Girl With The Dragon Tattoo, all proving that it's okay to be different.

It's not only actresses who are finding meatier roles these days, but also women writers and directors, who are stepping up to bat in record numbers.

I recently attended a SAG members screening of The Invisible Woman in Hollywood, followed by a chat with its stars Felicity Jones and Ralph Fiennes. It's Fiennes's second foray into directing and, while he plays a starring role as Charles Dickens, the story is really that of Dickens's mistress, Nelly Ternan. Felicity Jones was drawn to the project by a strong female role and Fiennes by Abi Morgan's screenplay. She won the Emmy last year for TV's The Hour and also wrote the screenplay for Oscar-winning biopic The Iron Lady.

Costas Sarkas

It's hard to feel that women in Hollywood are in a better position than ever when one comes across newspaper articles like one in December 2013 in The Observer. The naked truth: Hollywood still treats its women as second-class citizens. The article addressed a comprehensive study by the New York Film Academy on gender inequality in film. Its findings are highly indicative of there still being a very long way to go in countering the prevalence of male voices in Hollywood. It might indeed be true that more actresses are finding meatier roles nowadays but the numbers are still worryingly low: the study looked at the top 500 films between 2007 and 2012 to find that only 30.8 per cent of the speaking parts were filled by women and that only 10.7 per cent of movies featured

ABOVE: Costas Sarkas

Credit: Mark Boardman, www.mark-boardman.com